3-D ART LAB FOR KIDS

Susan Schwake

Photography by
RAINER SCHWAKE

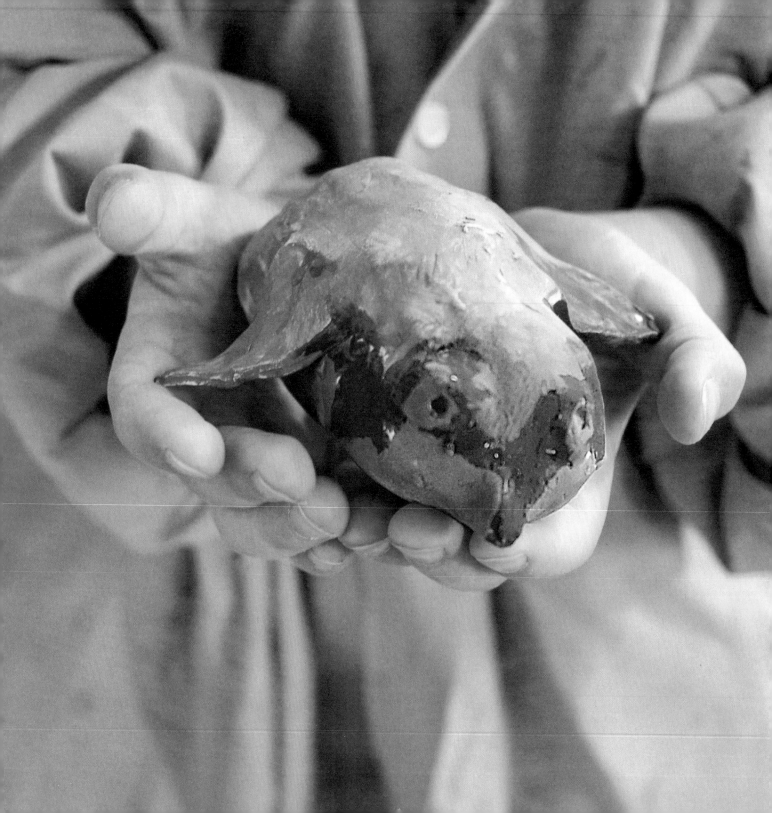

3-D ART LAB FOR KIDS

32 HANDS-ON ADVENTURES IN SCULPTURE AND MIXED MEDIA

Susan Schwake

PHOTOGRAPHY BY
RAINER SCHWAKE

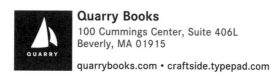

Quarry Books
100 Cummings Center, Suite 406L
Beverly, MA 01915
quarrybooks.com • craftside.typepad.com

First published in the United States of America in 2013 by
Quarry Books, a member of
Quayside Publishing Group
100 Cummings Center
Suite 406-L
Beverly, Massachusetts 01915-6101
Telephone: (978) 282-9590
Fax: (978) 283-2742
www.quarrybooks.com
Visit www.Craftside.Typepad.com for a behind-the-scenes peek at our crafty world!
Visit www.QuarrySPOON.com and help us celebrate food and culture one spoonful at a time!

10 9 8 7 6 5 4 3 2 1

ISBN: 978-1-59253-815-7
Digital edition published in 2013
eISBN: 978-1-61058-946-8

Library of Congress Cataloging-in-Publication Data

Schwake, Susan.
  3-D Art Lab for Kids : 32 hands-on adventures in sculpture and mixed media / Susan Schwake;
Photography by Rainer Schwake.
      pages cm
Summary: "An inspiring collection of ideas and projects for encouraging an artistic spirit in children!
3-D Art Lab for Kids includes 32 kid-friendly fine art projects in paper, clay, textiles, sculpture, and
jewelry. Each project is inspired by the work of a prominent artist and is illustrated with step-by-step
full-color photographs of the process as well as finished samples and variations. Whether you use
these projects independently or as a curriculum for hands-on 3-D art experiences, you'll find that
the lessons in this book are open-ended so they can be explored over and over-with different results
each time! Colorful photos illustrate how different people using the same lesson will yield different
results, exemplifying the way the lesson brings out each artist's personal style. 3-D Art Lab for Kids
is the perfect book for creative families, friends, and community groups and works as lesson plans
for both experienced and new art teachers. Children of all ages and experience levels can be guided
by adults and will enjoy these engaging exercises."-- Provided by publisher.
  ISBN 978-1-59253-815-7 (pbk.)
  1. Sculpture--Technique--Juvenile literature.
  2. Mixed media (Art)--Technique--Juvenile literature. I. Title.
  NB1170.S353 2013
  702.8--dc23
                                                    2013012624

Design: Rainer Schwake
All photography by Rainer Schwake with the exception of the following:
Chloe Larochelle, 144; James Lord, 139 (bottom right); Egbert Schwake, 5;
Susan Schwake, 140–141; Shutterstock.com 28, 77 (bottom); Trigger Image/Alamy, 105 (bottom)

Printed in China

This book is dedicated with love
to my husband, Rainer.

The creative man behind the scenes,
who really does make each of my
days better than the one before.

CONTENTS

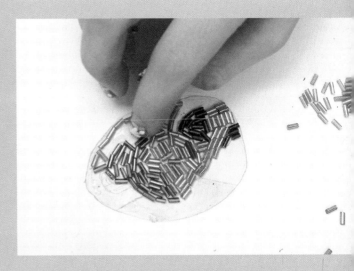

INTRODUCTION

This book is all about making art that pops out, stands up, swings from the ceiling, or makes you walk around it. My first real encounter with 3-D art was in a 3-D art and design class in college. My professor gave us our first assignment with paper. It was to take a flat piece of paper and make it into a sphere. I was a freshman and easily daunted—but this assignment rocked my world! (It also introduced me to the art of origami.)

Since that class, and other 3-D media courses I took in college, I have had the privilege to hone my 3-D skills under the guidance of some incredible artists and instructors. I transformed some of these experiences into lessons for my students and am pleased to share some of them inside these pages. It is my sincere hope that this book will inspire you to try your hand at making three-dimensional art and nurture that part of yourself that longs to mold material into your dream object.

Over the past twenty years of teaching, these lessons have emerged as the ones my students are "most likely to enjoy." Each lesson is inspired by an artist's work and meant to encourage each person's own style. In our gallery, I curate ten exhibits a year with groups of contemporary artists. My students view the work on a weekly basis in their classes. Along with these exhibits, my students are introduced to a broad range of art through books, slides, posters, and the Internet. However, nothing can replace seeing the actual artwork. I recommend visiting a local gallery or museum because walking around a piece of artwork or seeing a tapestry on the wall can be life changing.

1 SETTING UP

This book is for anyone interested in making art in 3-D, either with someone else or alone. There are so many materials, both found and specialty, that are perfect for art making in the round. The main point of this book is to inspire you to find new ways to use these materials and to make these lessons your own.

Taking a risk is part of working three-dimensionally. It's always a little tougher to get your art to stand up or stick out or hang from a ceiling. Go out on a limb and try your idea! It may not work the very first time, but with a little patience and a second try, it can be the best thing you have ever done. In this chapter, I outline what you will need to set up a studio and some ideas for working with others.

SOME IMPORTANT IDEAS ABOUT MAKING 3-D ART

Each person's work should be wholly his or her own. Don't work on someone else's art. Make your own. Use thoughtful language when working with others. For example, "Tell me about your idea" works better than "What is that?"

- Always use the best materials that you can for each art-making session.

- Don't worry about "wrecking" a new material. Usually it can be recycled into something new if you fall short of your goal.

- Promote fearlessness.

- Embrace individual style. Respect each other's work, even if you don't understand it.

The lessons in this book are starting points. They are meant to be used over and over again incorporating your own ideas into the exercise each time. The most important lessons in art are the ones that you discover about yourself in the process. Be brave, experiment, and fear no art!

SETTING UP A 3-D ART AREA

This section will prepare you for making 3-D art with children and keeping the mood and materials under control. These projects are a little more exciting and a little more physical, for the most part, than their 2-D cousins. I have created these lessons in my home, in my studio, and as an artist-in-residence in classes with up to thirty students.

The key to keeping it cool is preparation and experimentation. If you are teaching these lessons to children, I highly recommend trying them out first so you are comfortable with the medium. Do not be discouraged if your product does not match your expectations the first time around. Try it again, and after a few tries you should be more comfortable with your results. Most of all, remember that play is a big part of the process, and the process is everything. Results are secondary to the actual experience. With practice, your results will improve like all new adventures!

Setting Up for Working with Paper

Paper is a pretty "clean" material to work with; however, when you add water and glue, things can get a bit messy. Before starting any cutting project, I suggest laying out a large paper covering or thin plastic mat to catch some of the cuttings. Tape a lunch paper bag to the edge of the table where you are working to brush scraps out of the way of the art making.

For gluing paper and for making books, it is advisable to have freezer or waxed paper on hand. When slipped under the project during the gluing process, this layer creates a desirable nonstick surface. At the very least, a second piece of clean scrap paper should be used to protect the table from the glue application process. Replace this paper when it gets too sticky.

When working with papier-mâché, it is best to start with layers. A plastic table covering first and then a thick layer of newspaper will ensure the least mess. Layers of newspaper can become wet and incorporated into the art easily. A bowl for each student, or every two students, reduces the likelihood that someone will spill the "goo." Recycled plastic containers with a shallow, wide profile are best.

To create the goo follow this simple recipe: Start with a large bowl and fill it halfway with white flour. The cheaper the better! Pour in enough warm water to create a pastelike consistency when stirred. Continue stirring, and add more water until it has the consistency of heavy cream. That's it!

For folding paper, it is nice but not necessary to have a bone folder and a smooth, flat surface for folding. A firm finger or thumb can replace the bone folder. Bone folders can often be found at craft stores or stationery stores.

Hot glue should be used with supervision and a bowl of iced water nearby for safety.

Cutting thick cardboard may require adult hands if the cardboard is too stiff for smaller hands.

Setting Up for Working with Clay

Choose a place that is far from food, pets, and small children. If you don't have a sink nearby, you can always have a bucket of water for cleaning hands and paper towels for cleaning the table.

A waist-high table is best for working with clay. For wedging the clay and for modeling, your arms should be able to rest comfortably on the table without reaching or bending. Your work surface can be covered with a piece of canvas or a smooth board such as Masonite or smooth plywood. This keeps the clay from sticking. The board can also be used as a portable work surface to put your work away when you are finished for the day. It's a good idea to have a tiny container of water and a scoring tool for each student's work station—or shared between students.

For making slabs of clay, you will need a rolling pin or fat dowel to roll the clay out.

Using two slats of wood on either side of the clay will keep the slab an even thickness. At our studio, we make slabs as follows:

1. Start with a wedged slab of clay. Lay your wood strips to either side of the clay with the rolling pin touching both sides.
2. Start in the middle of the clay with your thumbs touching each other on top of the pin.
3. Roll back and forth—only in the middle— three or four times and then flip. You don't have to press very hard.
4. Continue until the clay is the thickness of the slats. Don't worry about the ends; they will flatten out as you flip.

If you don't have access to a kiln to fire your projects, you will need to find one. Local potters or paint-your-own-pottery shops will typically fire your pieces for a fee. Local community centers, schools, colleges, or camps may also have a kiln for hire. The first firing of bone-dry clay projects is called "bisque" firing, a process that forces all the remaining water from the clay, leaving it very hard and porous to accept the final glaze. The second firing is used to set the clear glaze and make the objects waterproof.

Setting Up for Textile Work

A comfortable chair and waist-high table are needed for any project. And good lighting is a must! When hand sewing, it is nice to have a small container for needles or pins to rest in. Threads, binding tape, and other notions can be kept tidy in resealable plastic bags or totes.

For weaving, it is easier for some people to work vertically on a wall. You can hammer a nail or two into the wall to hang your work from or use a piece of Homasote or corkboard to pin your project to while it is in process.

When working with textiles, you often need to know how to make a square knot. Simple instructions for making one follow.

1. Begin with an end of a string, strip of fabric, or trim in each hand.

2. Place the right string over the left and fold under.

3. Place the left string over the right and fold under.

4. Pull tight—there is your square knot!

Setting up for Working with Other Sculpture Materials

When making relief sculptures from joint compound, it is good to lay newspaper under your work to protect the table. A putty knife or painting knife is the tool that should touch the compound and the work—not your hands. That said, having a large, wet sponge nearby to wipe off inquisitive fingers is advised. Colored joint compounds are recommended for use with kids because their color fades as they dry, indicating that the "creating time" is nearing an end.

When making dioramas and small found-object art, it's best to have all the materials laid out on a table. Knowing what is available makes creating easier, and placing materials in small jam jars, baby food containers, and recycled plastic containers—all collected on trays—makes for ease of use, cleanup, and storage.

Setting Up for Making Jewelry

When creating with beads, it is advisable to have a tray under your work so stray beads do not roll away. I find Styrofoam trays handy, as well as small lunch trays or cookie sheets. If you purchase or recycle loose beads, keeping them in baby food jars or jam jars will keep them tidy and visable. Having your wire, beading thread, scissors, wire cutters, and benders together in a tote on the table before you begin is helpful too. Good lighting and a waist-high table are always advisable.

2 TOOLS OF THE TRADE

This chapter provides a master list of things that will make your art making more enjoyable. It is not necessary to have every item before you begin. Just gather what you already have and then add materials as you are able. Some of the lessons use household materials, while others incorporate more specialized artist's equipment. Please don't be intimidated by the list! It is meant to serve as a reference, not a requirement. I start with general studio items that are useful to have in your work space, followed by lists of special media for each of the lessons in the book.

General Materials

1. Copy paper for sketching out ideas.
2. Pencils, erasers, and sharpeners.
3. Oil pastels, paint markers, and colored pencils for adding color.
4. UHU glue sticks, clear liquid glue, fabric glue, and tacky glue.
5. Hot glue guns (low melt is safest) and sticks.
6. Containers for water in assorted sizes and heights. Recycled glass jars, plastic tubs, and small yogurt, applesauce, and cat food containers work well for many sorting needs.
7. Craft paper for table coverings and construction.
8. Good lighting, waist-high tables, and comfortable chairs. Sitting on your feet or knees makes it hard to stay steady.
9. Assorted papers in different weights, colors, and patterns. Recycled paper from junk mail, security envelopes, magazines, wrappers, and discarded books are wonderful choices.
10. A place to exhibit your finished 3-D pieces—a tabletop, shelf, or cabinet.
11. Basic tools: hammer, nails, wire cutters, scissors, craft knife (only to be used by an adult), and assortment of lightweight wire.

Paper

1. Newspaper for everything from construction to clay to covering surfaces.
2. Colored, acid-free paper for construction. Construction paper fades, but it can be used as a cheaper alternative.
3. Origami and specialty papers for covering constructions and book arts. There are so many colors and prints available, and they are beautiful when used on a range of applications.
4. Recycled paper: security envelopes, magazines, junk mail, candy and other wrappers, discarded book jackets, rejected artwork, old homework, and anything headed for the recycling bin!
5. Cardboard, corrugated or not, is good for providing structure or reinforcement, and it can also be used for relief building.
6. Cardboard boxes are essential for large papier-mâché work.
7. Tape of all kinds: colored paper tape, masking tape, cellophane tape, duct tape, and electrical tape.

Clay

1. The clay lessons in this book use earthenware clay rated to cone 06-04. These numbers are used as a guide for how hot to fire the clay. Either red or white clay is fine—or try mixing them for a swirled effect!

2. A variety of clay tools is nice to have, but it's fine to start with a single pin tool, which can score, draw, make holes, and do most everything to clay that your finger cannot. As you'll see in the clay section, we make a scoring tool, which is a great addition and cheap to make. It is simply a paint stirrer cut in half with eight straight pins epoxyed to one end. This tool was created by Megan Bogonovich and has helped all my students make good connections with their clay (see image). For making slabs, you need a wooden rolling pin and set of slats for making even slabs. If you dive deeply into clay, additional tools to have on hand include a wooden and rubber rib, fettling knife, hole maker, and tile cutters. These tools are not expensive, but you can use other household items in their place. For example, a plastic lid can be cut to resemble a rib and works fairly well, and a cookie cutter can work in place of a tile cutter.

3. Canvas pieces cut to at least 24 x 24 inches (61 x 61 cm) to work on.

4. Masonite or smooth plywood sheet to work on. Again, 24 x 24 inches (61 x 61 cm) is a good basic size.

5. A kiln or access to one.

6. Low-fire underglazes and a clear glaze to paint over it. These should be lead-free and nontoxic marked cone 06-04.

7. Paintbrushes: small for painting details and large for covering bigger areas.

8. Rulers for cutting straight lines.

9. Bowls and small sponges for scoring and smoothing.

10. Newspaper for keeping glazing area clean.

11. Clay cutter tool (either a wire or nylon string type).

12. Plastic bags to keep the clay soft and projects wet over a period of time.

13. Big bucket and sponge to clean the work space when project is finished.

14. Sponges for smoothing the work: small soft rounds, small soft sea sponges, and silk sponges. Available at all ceramic supply stores. Cosmetic sponges work in a pinch.

scoring tool

Textiles

1. Assortment of scraps and small yardage of fabrics for weaving, embellishments, and patches.
2. Lightweight canvas, muslin, or other light-colored fabrics for soft scultpures and embroidery work.
3. Yarns and strings of all sorts for weaving, soft sculpture hair, and other sculptural needs.
4. Sticks and lightweight lumber for making looms or stretching fabric.
5. Embroidery hoops.
6. Assortment of needles with large eyes, pins, and pincushion for stitching projects.
7. Fiberfill, kapok, or cotton batting for stuffing soft sculptures.
8. Birch bark, leaves, twigs, shells, and other bits of nature to weave and incorporate into sculptures.
9. Chopsticks for poking stuffing into place in soft sculptures.
10. Buttons, trims, and notions for embellishing textile work.
11. Acrylic paints and bristle paintbrushes for painting on fabric.
12. Adhesives: tacky glue, fabric glue, and hot glue.

Sculpture

1. Cardboard boxes, tubes, and panels for construction.
2. Watercolor and acrylic paint for finishing and adding color.
3. Joint compound for relief panels.
4. Wooden panels for construction and for substrate.
5. Beads, trims, notions, buttons, and discarded jewelry for embellishments.
6. Dried moss, scraps of wood, stumps, birch bark, acorns, and other bits of nature for found-object sculptures.
7. Astroturf, tiny plastic toys, faux flowers, and leaves for found-object sculptures.
8. Cigar boxes and small gift boxes.
9. Felt and fabric for puppet making.
10. Styrofoam shapes, thin dowels, wooden skewers, toothpicks, and Popsicle sticks.
11. Assortment of paper and tissue for finishing and adding color.
12. Hot glue, green florist tape and clay, tacky glue, and clear glue and tape.
13. Stemless wine glasses to use as vitrines for Little Worlds (see page 118).

Jewelry

1. Wire cutters and round wire pliers.
2. Assortment of beads, including small, medium, and seed style.
3. Waxed linen thread and memory wire.
4. Felt with adhesive backing for backing pins.
5. Surgical steel ear wires and jump rings.
6. Assortment of colorful papers and laminating sheets.
7. Colored pencils and card stock.
8. Clear liquid glue and glue sticks. I recommend UHU glue sticks as they last a long time and work extremely well.
9. 1-inch (2.5 cm) circle punch for making earring shapes.
10. Dimensional glue for adding accents and texture. I recommend Mod Podge Dimensional Magic.

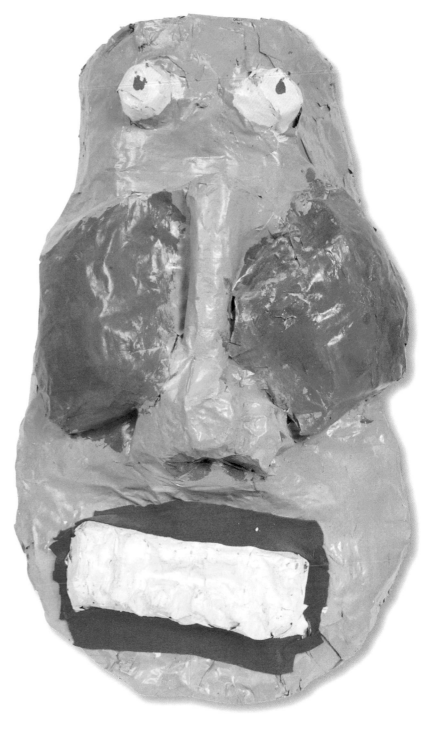

3 PAPER: TRANSFORMED

Paper is one of the most versatile materials. An artist can change the appearance of paper by adding color, water, or glue, or simply by folding it. It is readily available and is a material that I cannot imagine living without. Paper is most often made from plant fibers. The lessons in this chapter involve paper being transformed into three-dimensional objects. From handmade books to relief sculptures, paper is at the core of these lessons. We will use a wide variety of papers, from thick cardboard to thin origami paper, to create our sculptural objects.

Keep an eye out for special papers! Some come to you in the mail as colorful junk mail or the inside of security envelopes. Keep a box of recycled papers handy for this kind of project. Another great source for beautiful papers is a scrapbooking or art supply shop. There you may find inexpensively printed papers, more expensive handmade papers, and different weights of drawing or painting papers—all of which you can use to make 3-D work. Don't overlook copy paper, wrapping papers, or newsprint. They each have a place in the 3-D art studio.

RAINSTICKS

Before You Begin

It's fun to make an instrument that you can play. This lesson does just that. Do a little research on the history of the rain stick at your local library or online. Today rain sticks are used as instruments in Mexican and South American music. Find recordings of this kind of music and play along after your rain stick is finished. Or make up your own song!

MATERIALS

- paper tube: at least 12 inches (30 cm) long and 2.5 inches (6 cm) wide (mailing tubes work well)
- hammer
- common nails shorter than the diameter of your tube
- dried beans
- masking tape
- flour, water, and bowl for making papier-mâché goo
- newspaper
- jute
- white glue
- waxed paper
- acrylic paint and paintbrushes
- optional: paint markers

LET'S GO!

1. Begin by hammering the nails in a pattern around your tube from the top to the bottom (fig. 1).

2. Put on the bottom lid and add three or four handfuls of dried beans to the tube (fig. 2).

3. Put on the top lid and tape both lids shut if they are not secure. Blend the papier-mâché goo by adding enough flour by the handful to water to make a liquid as thick as cream. Stir with your hand or a spoon. (See "Setting Up for Working with Paper" in chapter 1.)

4. Tear the newspaper into small strips and place the paper in a bowl or box to keep dry (fig. 3).

5. Dip the paper strips into the mixture and scrape off any excess with two fingers (fig. 4).

6. Smooth the wet paper onto the tube. Begin at the bottom and work to the top if your tube is tippy. Wait to cover the bottom lid until the end (fig. 5).

(1) Hammer the nails.

(2) Add the beans.

(3) Tear the newspaper.

(4) Dip the strips.

(5) Smooth the strips.

(6) Cover the top.   (7) Cover the bottom lid.

7. Continue until you reach the top lid and cover the top completely (fig. 6).

8. Flip over the tube and finish by covering the bottom lid (fig. 7).

9. Let the tube dry completely. This may take a day or two, depending on the weather.

10. Cut some sections of jute and glue them in a decorative pattern around the tube with the white glue. This gives texture and grip when playing the stick (fig. 8).

11. Papier-mâché over the jute and let dry (fig. 9).

12. Use acrylic paint to cover your rain stick with color and create patterns as desired (fig. 10).

13. Detail your rain stick with paint markers and/or acrylic paint using small paintbrushes (fig. 11).

(8) Add the jute.

(9) Papier-mâché over the jute.

(10) Paint the rainstick.

(11) Detail the rainstick.

BE INSPIRED

Traditional rainsticks are made from cactus and are believed to have originated in Chile or Peru. The native peoples believed that playing the rainsticks would help bring rainstorms to their dry areas. They are also used today as musical instruments.

Traditional-style cactus rainstick

KEEP GOING!

Try making a few different sizes of rainsticks to hear the difference between them. You could even start a rainstick band!

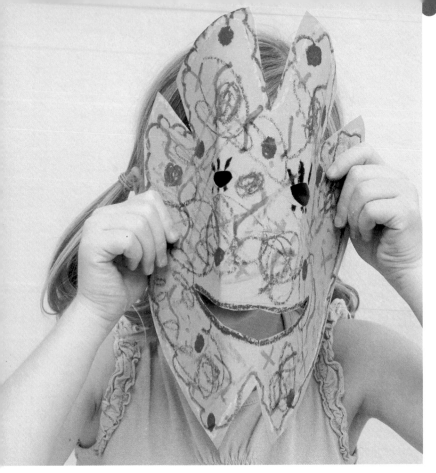

PAPER MASKS

Before You Begin

Masks are found throughout the world in all cultures. Masks can show emotions, celebrate life's passages, or simply be for fun. This easy-to-make mask can be used over and over as a base for a simple or more complex mask. Think about what you want to say with your mask and then choose embelishments and color to convey your idea.

MATERIALS

- pattern (see page 33)
- card stock in assorted colors
- pencil
- scissors
- oil pastels or paint markers
- masking tape
- colored tape
- assortment of embellishments (see master list)
- clear liquid glue or glue stick
- hole punch
- elastic cord or yarn

(1) Trace the pattern.

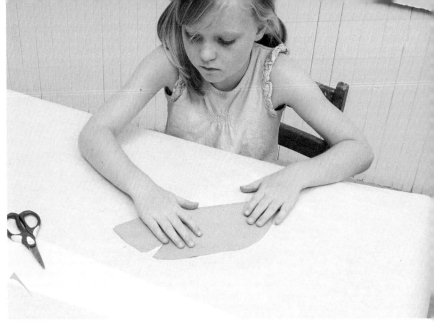

(2) Cut out the mask.

(3) Fold lengthwise.

LET'S GO!

1. Enlarge the pattern from page 33, or simply draw a similar one.

2. Trace around the pattern with a pencil on the colored card stock (fig. 1).

3. Cut out the mask (fig. 2).

4. Fold the mask in half lengthwise (fig. 3).

5. Cut out a mouth in the bottom third of the mask on the fold (fig. 4).

(4) Cut the mouth.

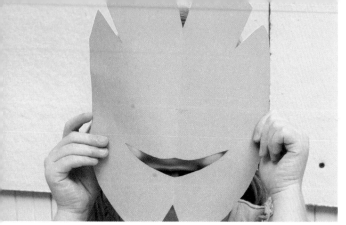

(5) Open mask and add color.

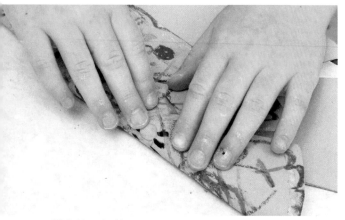

(6) Fold each side.

6. Open up the mask and begin adding your color with oil pastels or markers (fig. 5).

7. Fold each side of the mask into the middle fold (fig. 6).

8. Draw the eyes in, centered on the fold, with a pencil. Then cut them out on the fold you just made (fig. 7).

9. Open the mask and try it on

10. Fold over the sides of the slits to shape the mask around your chin and forehead with masking tape on the inside of the mask (fig. 8).

(7) Cut the eye holes on the fold.

(8) Tape the slits.

(9) Tape the front of the mask.

11. Embellish the outside slits with colored tape and add any further details with clear glue or a glue stick (fig. 9).

12. Punch a hole on each side of the mask to attach the cord for wearing the mask. Use elastic cord or yarn tied to the hole.

KEEP GOING!

You can make your mask out of different materials. Try heavyweight felt or fabric and use hot glue or fabric glue for your embellishments. You might try stitching on the fabric for details.

BE INSPIRED

Masks: Faces of Culture
by John W. Nunley and Cara McCarty

This book is a wonderful collection of masks from around the globe.

Photocopy at 200%.

PAPER BEAD FIGURES

Before You Begin

Think about who your figure might be before you start. It can be anyone you dream up, a historical figure, or perhaps a rock star! You are the artist, so you choose.

MATERIALS

- pipe cleaners (three per figure)
- colorful magazine pages
- wooden skewers or tiny dowel
- glue stick
- Mod Podge and small brush
- card stock
- pencil
- fine-line markers
- wooden beads with holes big enough to pass pipe cleaners through
- tacky glue
- paper clay or earthenware clay
- acrylic paint and paintbrushes

(1) Twist pipe cleaners together.

(2) Form the arms and hands.

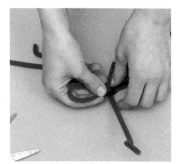

(3) Shape the head.

4. Cut out long triangles of colorful magazine pages as shown. Coat one side with the glue stick and roll them around a skewer or tiny dowel (fig. 4).

5. Slide beads of the skewer. When you have a pile of one to two dozen beads, coat them lightly with Mod Podge to seal (fig. 5).

LET'S GO!

1. Lay two pipe cleaners on a table to form an X. Twist them together to form a body (fig. 1).

2. Above the twist, shape the pipe cleaners into arms and hands (fig. 2).

3. Cut another pipe cleaner in half for the head. Twist the ends together to form a neck and twist it onto the body (fig. 3).

(4) Make paper beads.

(5) Coat the beads.

35

6. Make the face of your figure. Lay the pipe cleaner body on a piece of card stock. Using a pencil, trace around the head to create a face. Do this a second time to create the back of the head. Draw a face on the front and hair on the back with the fine-line markers and then cut out the two pieces (fig. 6).

7. You can make the shirt or torso, both front and back, in the same manner as the front and back of the head and as shown in these examples (fig 7).

8. When the paper beads are dry, you can begin constructing your figure. Put the legs together and run one or two of your beads up to the neck to form the torso (fig. 8).

9. Use the paper beads and the wooden beads to fill in the arms and the legs (fig. 9).

10. Attach the paper face, back of head, and front and back of the shirt using tacky glue (fig. 10).

(6) Make the head.

(7) Make the shirt.

(8) Make the torso.

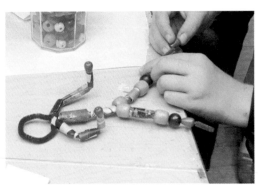

(9) Fill in the arms and legs.

(10) Glue on the paper parts.

11. Create a base from the clay of your choice that is thick enough to hold the figure upright. It can be any shape you wish. Poke holes in the base to hold your figure in position. Make the holes slightly larger than the pipe cleaner as the clay will shrink as it dries. Let the clay dry and paint it as desired. If you use earthenware clay, you must fire it before painting it (fig. 11).

12. Put a few drops of tacky glue in the base holes before placing your figure inside. Prop up the figure if needed until dry (fig. 12).

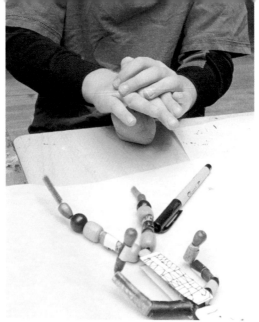
(11) Make the base.

KEEP GOING!

You can make as many figures as you can dream up. How about an entire baseball team or rock band? You can also try making your favorite animal or a whole zoo!

(12) Place the figure in the base.

MEET THE ARTIST: ALBERTO GIACOMETTI

Alberto Giacometti is my favorite sculptor. Here is a photo of me standing next to a sculpture of his at the Museum of Modern Art in New York City. Read about this famous sculptor at your local library or at the Giacometti Foundation website, www.fondation-giacometti.fr.

The author at the Museum of Modern Art in New York City

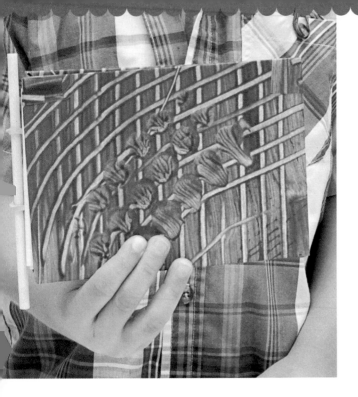

STICK-BOUND SKETCHBOOK

Before You Begin

It's fun to make your very own book. You can use some of your discarded paintings for the book covers or paint a new cover before you start the project. Any medium-weight paper will do. Think about using two different papers—one for the outside covers and one for inside the covers. They can be in the same color families or contrasting in color. You are the artist, so you may choose! You can also make books of varying sizes once you become familiar with the process.

LET'S GO!

1. Place the mat board on top of one of the smaller pieces (11 x 7 inches [28 x 18 cm]) of decorative paper. Trace around the mat board with a pencil. This will be your fold line. Using the ruler, measure out 1 inch (2.5 cm) all around your fold line and draw a second line. This will be your cutting line (fig. 1).

2. Cut out the cover following your cutting line (fig. 2).

3. Using the ruler, draw a triangle at each of the corners as shown (fig. 3).

4. Cut off the corners at the line you just drew (fig. 4).

5. Using the glue stick, liberally apply the glue to the back of the paper making sure you go around the edges (fig. 5). Use a piece of newspaper under your paper to keep things neat.

6. Line your mat board up on the paper according to the fold lines you drew (fig. 6).

(1) Measure for the cutting line.

(2) Cut out the outside covers.

(3) Mark the corners.

(4) Cut off the corners.

(5) Apply the glue.

(6) Line up the paper.

(7) Fold the edges.

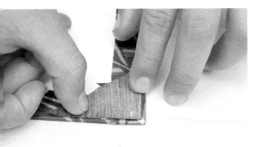

(8) Cover the corners.

(9) Glue the inside cover.

(10) Lay in the pages.

7. Press the mat board onto the paper and fold up the edges all around (fig. 7).

8. If you have a gap at the corners, don't worry! Simply cut out a triangle to cover the corners. Even if you don't have a gap, you might want to do this just for decoration (fig. 8).

9. Now it's time to glue the inside cover to the outside covers using the long piece of decorative paper that will hinge the two covers together. Lay out the 20-inch (51 cm) length of decorative paper and coat the back side liberally with the glue stick. Carefully line up the inside cover with the outside covers, placing them a little less than 1 inch (2.5 cm) apart as shown. Press firmly to form a solid bond (fig. 9).

10. Place the twelve pages of sketch paper inside the book. They should be lined up evenly from the center (fig. 10).

11. Flip the stack over so the outside covers are facing up and the sketch pages are underneath. Use a clothespin or bull clip if you find that the pages and covers are moving around too much. Using the screw punch, put two holes in the sketchbook pages between the two covers. They should be placed about 1½ inches (4 cm) from the top and bottom edges (fig. 11).

12. Open your book to the middle, and thread one side of the rubber band through the top hole and the other side through the bottom hole.

13. Flip the book over carefully and wrap the top of the rubber band around the top of the stick and slide it through the bottom of the rubber band as shown (fig. 12).

14. Open your book and gently turn the pages one at a time to help them lie flat.

(11) Punch the holes.

(12) Bind the stick to the book.

KEEP GOING!

The measurements in this lesson are completely flexible. You can make different sizes of books as long as you keep to the proportions provided above for the mat board, decorative paper, and sketch paper. Try making a sketchbook for a friend or fill one with photographs.

MEET THE ARTIST: GAIL SMUDA

Gail Smuda is a New Hampshire artist who works primarily with books, fiber, and mixed media. Often she combines them all. Shown here is her work called *Els Anne Dreams*. Learn more about Gail at www.gailsmuda.com.

Els Anne Dreams by Gail Smuda

41

CARDBOARD RELIEF PAINTING

Before You Begin

Relief sculpture can be made from many different media. Sometimes relief is carved from stone or plaster while other times it is created with wood or clay. This lesson uses cardboard, which is inexpensive and readily available, with hot glue. We chose a landscape for our subject matter, but you can pick any subject and it will work perfectly with this lesson.

MATERIALS

- assortment of cardboard pieces
- pencil
- scissors
- wood substrate (smooth plywood or Masonite up to ½-inch [13 mm] thick)
- hot glue gun and glue sticks
- acrylic paint and paintbrushes
- optional: paint markers, clear coat varnish

(1) Draw on the cardboard.

LET'S GO!

1. Begin by drawing your subject on the cardboard pieces with pencil (fig. 1).

2. Cut out each element and stack them on the wood substrate to arrange as shown (fig. 2).

3. Using the hot glue, attach your cardboard pieces to the base, starting with the pieces that will appear farthest away in your picture. Then add the elements that will appear closer by stacking them on top of the pieces you've already glued in place (fig. 3).

(2) Cut and stack the cardboard.

(3) Glue down the cardboard.

4. Use the hot glue to make raised details on top of your cardboard (fig. 4).

5. Let the glue dry for five minutes (fig. 5).

6. Paint the relief with the acrylic paints to color and seal the entire artwork (fig. 6).

(4) Add hot glue details.

(5) Wait for the glue to dry.

(6) Paint the relief.

7. If you'd like, add more details with paint markers (fig. 7).

8. You may choose to seal the relief with a spray clear coat varnish. This should be done outside by an adult.

(7) Add details.

KEEP GOING!

Try making a portrait of your pet in this manner.

MEET THE ARTIST: POLLY COOK

Polly Cook fell in love with clay when she took her first pottery class at age ten in an art center in Nashville, Tennessee. "Sculpting, carving, drawing, and painting with underglazes is a natural medium for my visual storytelling," she says. "I love creating scenes that are part of a larger story that others can interpret as their own." Love, childhood, loss, longing, and ordinary, daily adventures are just some of the themes she is drawn to. "A few of the artists I admire and am influenced by are Munch, Edward Hopper, and the German realists of the 1920s." Polly makes relief sculptures as large as giant murals! Read more about her at www.pollycook.com.

Echo, a low-relief ceramic on wood by Polly Cook

ROLLED PAPER RELIEF

Before You Begin

Making a relief sculpture out of rolled paper is not only inexpensive but can also be repeated over and over with different results each time. The paper rolls in our student's work are left flat, but they could be bent to add more angles if desired. If you use origami paper, it is already the right size. It is easy to cut squares of paper from assorted scraps or junk mail to complete this lesson too!

LET'S GO!

1. Roll each piece of paper into a tube. Use the glue stick to secure the shape (fig. 1).

MATERIALS

- small squares of decorative paper such as origami paper cut to about 6 inches (15 cm)
- glue stick
- mat board
- clear glue

(1) Roll the tubes.

2. Arrange the tubes on the mat board in whatever composition you'd like (fig. 2).

3. Glue pieces down beginning at the bottom and build up. Let dry (fig. 3).

4. Add more pieces with glue, building on your first layer (fig. 4).

5. When adding pieces at an angle, press firmly and hold for a few minutes until the glue is tacky and can grab the piece securely (fig. 5).

(2) Create the composition.

(3) Glue the first layer.

KEEP GOING!

Try using the rolls to make a flower garden. Cut the paper or rolls into different lengths.

(4) Build up the layers.

(5) Hold the tube in place.

BE INSPIRED

Paper has been rolled into tubes and used artfully for centuries. Origami is folded paper, but short widths of paper can be rolled and glued into "paintings" using a process called quilling. Quilling—and origami—inspired this lesson. Why not go further and try mixing all three of these processes? For more information on quilling, visit http://en.wikipedia.org/wiki/quilling.

POTTER JANE KAUFMANN

Jane Kaufmann is a New Hampshire state treasure. She is a beloved artist who has worked in her studio for forty years making raku sculptures from tiny finger puppets to large-scale carved pedestals with huge figures on top. I am thrilled to share this visit we had at her studio.

What can you tell us about your beginnings as a maker?
I took classes at the University of New Hampshire. When a secondhand kiln came on the market for $150, I bought it and started making clay things at home.

How did you start making sculptures?
I took a sculpture class from Art Balderacchi. We were casting Styrofoam in wet sand. He wouldn't let the women hold the crucible, so I started making 3-D sculptures on the top of old paintings and large sculptures out of Styrofoam covered with modeling paste.

What are your favorite materials to use?
Paper, found materials, watercolor.

Who are your favorite artists?
Gauguin, Schiele, Hundertwasser, Calder.

What was your proudest moment?
When I drove to a function this morning in Rye, New Hampshire, for Dody Kolb, who used to run the Wentworth-Coolidge Gallery, in the fog without getting into an accident. I can't see well anymore, and it was a real effort.

More information about Jane can be found at www.janekaufmann.com

4 CLAY PLAY

Working with clay is an exciting, physical kind of art-making process. Little children know right away what they want to do with it. There are lots of different kinds of clay, and choosing which to use can be daunting. We work with low-fire clay in both white and red with excellent results and so this is what is used in this book. The colorful underglazes we suggest give children (and adults!) much freedom of expression and predictable results in their work.

I truly think that the experience of working with clay helps to develop better drawing skills and other 2-D work for students. Once you understand a shape in your hand—"in the round" —you are better able to render it in 2-D. And the thrill of making a cup or bowl with your own two hands is a wonderful thing! There are more steps when working with clay and more chances for things not to work out, but with a few simple rules you will have great success. So dive in and get a little muddy—the physical nature of clay will captivate you!

PINCH POTS

Before You Begin

Pinch pots may be one of the oldest forms of pottery. The only tools you need are your own two hands, and the results can be so varied that you might not recognize that the finished piece was made from pinching! It is a versatile method, and once you get the hang of it, you won't want
to stop making pinch pots. This lesson will make a basic pot. You can use it for holding small objects on a desk or cotton balls in the bathroom or make it a sugar bowl for your kitchen! There is no end to what you can make with the pinch method.

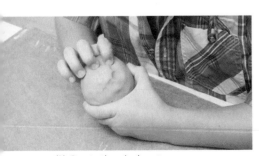

(1) Roll a smooth ball.

LET'S GO!

1. Begin with a ball of clay that fits in your hand comfortably (fig. 1).

2. Insert your dominant hand's thumb almost all the way through—but not through the bottom (fig. 2).

3. Work the ball of clay on your thumb with your index and middle fingers pinching the clay from the bottom around in a spiral motion to the top (fig. 3). Keep the hole small!

(2) Push your thumb in.

(3) Create the pinch pot.

MATERIALS

- canvas or wooden board to work on
- low-fire clay
- texture tools
- letter stamps
- low-fire underglazes
- soft clay sponge or natural sponge
- optional: clear, food-safe glaze

(4) Make the walls even.

(5) Add texture.

(6) Add letters.

4. As you work your way up to the rim, try to keep the hole small. It's easy to make it bigger later but hard to make it smaller.

5. Finish the pot by making sure that the walls are the same thickness from the top to the bottom and all the way around (fig. 4).

6. Remember that your pot has thin walls and needs support when adding the texture. Use one hand to press your tool into the outside of the clay, and place your other hand inside to support the clay walls (fig. 5).

7. You can use rubber stamps with letters to add your name if you like (fig. 6). Let dry and fire.

8. Using an underglaze, paint the inside and outside of the pot. If you'd like, use a small, damp sponge to remove some glaze and expose the texture (fig. 7).

9. To make it food safe, glaze with a clear, food-safe glaze and fire again.

(7) Add the glaze.

MEET THE ARTIST: CADA DRISCOLL

Cada Driscoll is an artist and arts educator who lives and creates in Portland, Maine. She enjoys the simple elegance of pinch bowls and loves the feel of clay between her fingers. Cada is passionate about influencing people to be creative, unique, and self-assured through the creative arts and throughout all aspects of life. Learn more about Cada here: www.cadacreates.blogspot.com.

KEEP GOING!

- Make a set of Japanese-style teacups for your home, personalized with each family member's name.
- Make three different-size pots that can fit or nest inside each other.

MOOD MASKS

Before You Begin

Masks are found in all cultures of the world, dating back
to the earliest peoples. There are many different reasons
for making masks. These masks are small and decorative
wall sculptures that can convey any feeling that you wish.
Take a look in a mirror and notice where your eyebrows
are when you are smiling. Now make a frown. Where do
they go? Act surprised! What shape is your mouth and
where are those eyebrows of yours? Remember that when
making your mask.

MATERIALS

- canvas or wooden board to
  work on
- paper and pencil for sketching
- low-fire clay
- rolling pin and slat guides
- clay knife
- newspaper
- scoring tool
- low-fire underglazes
- optional: clear glaze, rubber-
  tipped tools for ceramics

(1) Roll out a slab of clay.

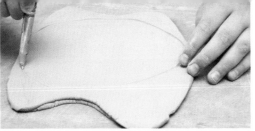

(2) Make the outline.

(3) Cut out the face.

LET'S GO!

1. Begin by making a drawing of your mask or by taking 2 pounds (900 g) of clay and rolling it out (fig. 1).

2. Remember to flip and then turn the clay 90 degrees each time you roll.

3. Lightly draw an outline of the face with your pencil or rubber-tipped tool, following your drawing if you made one (fig. 2).

4. Cut around the line with a clay knife (fig. 3).

5. Smooth the edges gently with your finger (fig. 4).

6. Make a small ball of newspaper and rest the clay on it to give it some curve—just like your real face (fig. 5).

7. Begin making the nose. Shape a length of clay the size of your middle finger or fatter into a tubelike shape.

8. Tap one end of the nose on the table to give it more of a snoutlike shape (fig. 6).

(4) Smooth the edges.

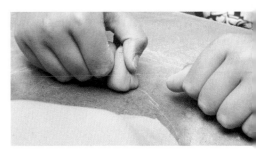

(5) Curve the face.

(6) Shape the nose.

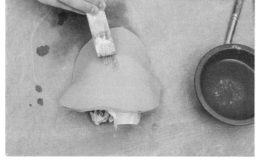

(7) Score the nose.

(8) Score the face.

(9) Smooth the nose.

10

11

12

13

9. Score the back of the nose and the area of the face where you want the nose to go. Attach the nose and smooth the edges onto the face (figs. 7, 8, 9). (See chapter 2 for scoring tips.) Remember to support the back of the slab (the underside of the face) with your other hand.

10. Poke a pencil or the small, rounded end of a tool into the nose to create nostrils (fig. 10).

11. Make the eyes from two small, like-size (or not!) balls of clay. Shape them as you wish and tap their back side to flatten. Score the flattened side (fig. 11).

12. Score the face and attach the eyes (fig. 12).

13. Now make the eyebrows. Roll two coils of clay on the board or between your hands to create expressive eyebrows. Flatten the back side and attach with scoring lines as before. You can make them hairy looking, if you like, with a pencil or the scoring tool (fig. 13).

14. Make the mouth from two coils of clay—one for the top lip and one for the bottom lip. Score them and create whatever expression you choose for your mouth and then attach them to the face. Smooth the connecting lines to make a good seal (fig. 14).

(14) Make the lips.

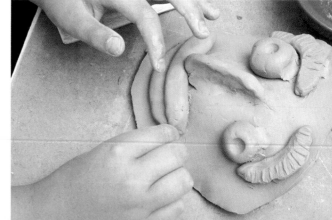

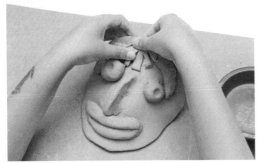
(15) Make some hair.

(16) Glaze the mask.

15. You can add hair at the forehead or a mustache or beard, but be careful not to have too many thin or long pieces sticking out from the face because they can easily break (fig. 15).

16. Let the mask dry and bisque fire. Using the underglaze, paint your mask the colors of your choice (fig. 16). Remember, color can add a lot of visual punch to your mood mask. It can also reflect a mood—blue is considered "sad", while red can be "angry." What color is your mood?

17. Add clear, shiny glaze and fire again, if desired, or just fire again without the glaze for a matte look.

scoring tool

MEET THE ARTIST: JEANNÉ McCARTIN

Jeanné McCartin has practiced sculpture for more than thirty years. Her work is driven by a fascination for the psychological underpinnings of human behavior. "You simply can't exhaust the subject," Jeanné says. "It's an exploration into what we reveal and what we hide and why we make those choices." Jeanné lives in New Hampshire.

Reveal by Jeanné McCartin

KEEP GOING!

Try making a mask of everyone in your family and hang them up together.

Masks can be hung near an entryway to greet visitors.

TEXTURES, STAMPS, AND TILES

Before You Begin

Have you ever looked at the mark your fingerprint makes after it's been pushed into soft clay? You can see the swirls and lines it makes. You can make a tool from clay that you can then use to add texture and interest to your other clay work. When you make an indent into clay and push other clay into it—and then pull it out— you are left with a raised impression of that indent. Try it! Now that you know how it works, figure out a pattern that you would like to make into a stamp tool all your own! Prepare to be amazed at what your tile will look like!

MATERIALS

- canvas or wooden board to work on
- low-fire clay
- assorted mark-making tools
- pencil, loop tools, texture plates, straws, and lace
- rolling pin and slat guides
- clay knife or square cookie cutters
- low-fire underglaze
- soft clay sponge or natural sponge
- clear glaze
- optional: kitchen scale (for measuring clay)

(1) Make the tube stamp.

LET'S GO!

1. Begin by creating a tube of clay a little thicker than the size of your index finger (fig. 1).

2. Using your mark-making tools (see chapter 2 for lots of ideas), begin patterning the tube of clay (fig. 2).

3. Continue around the tube stamp until you are satisfied (fig. 3).

4. Create a pattern on each end of the stamp. We used a walnut shell for this design (fig. 4).

5. Make sure that all of your tiny clay shards are gently rubbed off the marks.

6. Let dry and bisque fire to harden. Now you're ready to use your stamp!

(2) Mark the stamp.

(3) Continue making indentions.

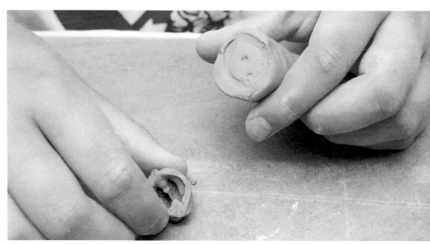
(4) Create patterned ends.

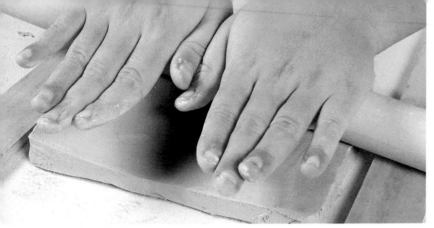

(5) Roll out the clay.

(6) Press in the stamp.

(7) Coat the tile with glaze.

7. Roll out a 1-pound (approx. 500 g) slab of clay as shown in chapter 2 (fig. 5).

8. Using a firm but not overly firm hand, press your new stamps into the clay (fig. 6).

9. Using a clay knife or small cookie cutters, cut out your desired tile shapes.

10. Make holes if desired, let them dry, and bisque fire.

11. Using the underglaze on the bisque-fired clay, coat the side of the tile that faces up (fig. 7).

Keep Going!

The texture tools you make need not be limited to rolling tubes. They can be squares or any shape you can think up.

Remember: If you choose to carve words or numbers in your tool, they must be created in reverse!

Make some tiles for your bathroom or kitchen wall.

12. Using a damp sponge, wipe away some of the glaze to expose the color of the clay (fig. 8).

13. Coat with the final clear glaze and fire again (fig. 9).

(8) Partially wipe away glaze to expose texture.

(9) Finish the tiles.

MEET THE ARTIST: MEGAN BOGONOVICH

Megan Bogonovich's work often has repeated patterns and textural details beyond what you can imagine. Each of her sculptures and the functional ware she makes demands different tools, so she makes them as she goes along. These are tiles that she made using some of her texture tools. Megan lives and works in Concord, New Hampshire, with her husband, Chuck.

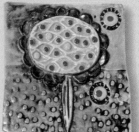

Texture tiles by Megan Bogonovich

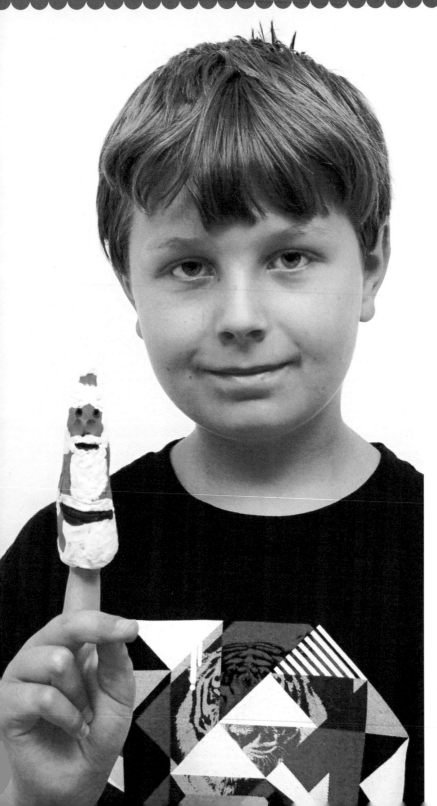

FINGER PUPPETS

Before you Begin

Try sketching a few different ideas of what your puppet might be. Our lesson is directly inspired by New Hampshire artist Jane Kaufmann, who has made almost every imaginable kind of puppet! Moose, angels, artists, mermaids, Santa Claus, scuba divers, gardeners, banditos, cows, and chefs are just a few of her signature puppets. The nice thing about the puppets is that they are miniature sculptures when they are not on your finger. I have a set of Jane's puppets that are modeled after Anthony and Cleopatra—complete with an asp. Think up your own puppet now!

MATERIALS

- canvas or wooden board to work on
- low-fire clay
- pencil or rubber-tipped tool
- low-fire underglazes and assorted soft paintbrushes
- optional: texture tools, clear glaze

(1) Shape the clay.

LET'S GO!

1. Begin by rolling a small ball of clay into a sausagelike shape (fig. 1).

2. Using your thumb or other finger, make a hole in the bottom of the puppet. This is where your finger will go. Remember that clay shrinks, so move your finger around inside the clay to open it up a little (fig. 2).

3. Smooth out all the cracks if any have occurred (fig. 3).

4. Pinch in a nose where the face will be (fig. 4).

(2) Make the hole.

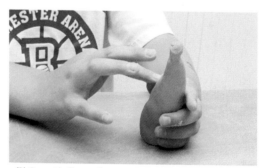

(3) Smooth the surface.

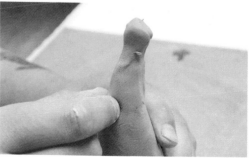

(4) Pinch in the nose.

5. Draw details with your pencil or rubber-tipped tool. Don't go too deep. You may also use your texture tools to add texture for hair, fur, and the like (fig. 5).

(5) Draw in the details.

6. When drawing in wet clay, you must gently brush away the crumbs (fig. 6).

7. When the clay dries, bisque fire the puppet. Add colorful underglazes to finish the detailing (fig. 7).

8. If you wish to have a shiny finish, you can add the clear glaze now before the final firing.

(6) Carefully brush away the crumbs.

(7) Paint with glaze.

KEEP GOING!

Make ten puppets—one for each finger!

Model a set of puppets after your family or group of friends.

MEET THE ARTIST: JANE KAUFMANN

Jane Kaufmann is a beloved and celebrated New England artist. I am honored to call her my friend. Of her work she says, "I make whatever comes into my mind. I am not influenced by what is currently fashionable in art magazines. I get ideas from the newspapers, books, my friends, Harper's magazine, tabloids, and anything else that I like. I believe and I do not believe everything I read. To me, things are simple and clear.

To learn more about Jane, visit her website, www.janekaufmann.com.

SHAKERS AND RATTLES

Before You Begin

Clay shakers have been part of many cultures' history dating back to Greek and Roman times. In North America, they are found in different tribes as musical instruments. Historically, babies are given rattles as toys, and there are plenty of rock bands that use shakers for their rhythm section. These clay shakers are fun to make and fun to play with when they are finished. Think a little about the decoration you will add at the end—texture- or smooth-glazed designs!

(1) Roll the clay ball in your hands.

LET'S GO!

1. Begin with a medium-size ball of clay that fits easily inside your palm. In addition, have an amount of clay (about the size of a golf ball) that will be made into the tiny rattlers that will go inside the shell (fig. 1).

MATERIALS

- canvas or wooden board to work on
- low-fire clay
- pin tool
- low-fire velvet underglazes
- optional: texture tools, clear glaze

2. Make the tiny balls that will be put inside the shell. Make as many as you can and keep them tiny (fig. 2).

3. From the remainder of the clay, form a smooth ball. Hold the ball in your hand. Using the thumb of your dominant hand, push it almost to the bottom of the ball (fig. 3).

4. Work the ball of clay on your thumb with your index and middle fingers pinching the clay from the bottom around in a spiral motion to the top (fig. 4). Keep the hole small!

5. Continue until there is a uniform thickness around the pot to the top (which is upside down when it's on your thumb, remember!).

(2) Make the rattlers.

(3) Begin making the pinch pot.

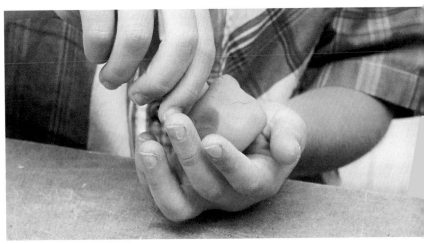

(4) Keep the opening small.

Clay Play   67

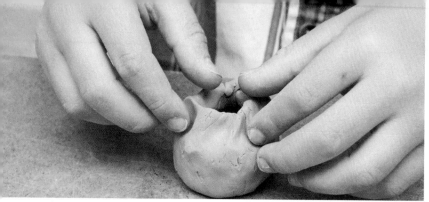

(5) Fold in the rim.

(6) Drop in the rattlers.

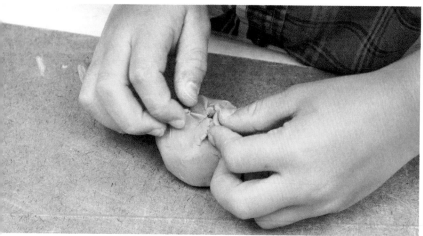

(7) Close the hole.

6. Because this is a closed vessel, we will now start to pinch the pot shut. Folding the clay in small sections around the rim, begin to make the opening smaller (fig. 5).

7. When it is almost closed, drop in the rattlers. They should be a little dry as they have been out since the beginning of the project (fig. 6).

8. Finish folding in the rim to create a little point, if you like, or simply shape the top as you wish (fig. 7). Remember that this is a hollow object and cannot take a lot of pressure. You can gently add texture now too, if desired.

9. When it is closed, take a pin tool and make a hole through the clay so it won't break in the kiln. Then set it aside to dry (fig. 8).

10. Bisque fire the shaker. You can underglaze it with your own designs (fig. 9).

11. Add a clear glaze and a final firing if desired—or leave matte. Now get shakin'!

(8) Make a hole through the clay before firing.

(9) Glaze the shaker.

KEEP GOING!

Make a variety of sizes of shakers—all with different amounts of rattlers inside.

Try making the shakers look like different fruits or vegetables as I did!

MEET THE AUTHOR: SUSAN SCHWAKE

I made a few shakers from porcelain in the shapes of unknown squash and even a little person! I like to pull them out to play with from time to time—and have used them for subject matter in painting still lifes with my students.

Pod shakers by Susan Schwake

WALL POCKETS

Before You Begin

These wall pockets can be quite functional. You can use them for storing pencils and paper for notes, to plant herbs, or even to stash your keys. Think about what sort of design you would like to have before you begin.

MATERIALS

· white stoneware clay
· rolling pin
· slab slats
· clay knife
· assortment of texture tools (These can be ones you have made or any object that you would like to press into your clay to add texture.)
· scoring tool
· small dish of water
· newspaper
· hole maker, pencil, or pin tool
· low-fire glazes
· assortment of paintbrushes

LET'S GO!

1. Roll out your clay in a slab, as outlined in chapter 2. Make it long and narrow.

2. Cut the edges cleanly with your slats and a clay knife (fig 1).

3. This piece will serve as the back of the pocket. Start adding texture to this piece with your tools. The bottom half of your slab will be inside the pocket, so you don't have to texture that part (fig. 2).

4. Score along the edges of the bottom half of the slab, dipping your scoring tool in water as you go to make a nice, wet score line (fig. 3).

(1) Cut the edges clean.

(2) Add textured designs.

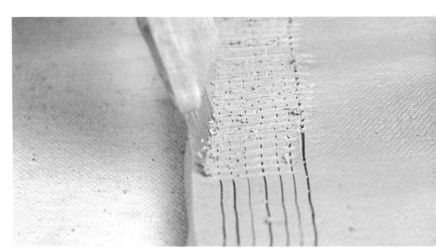

(3) Score the edges.

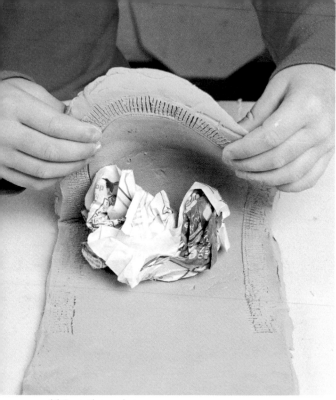

(4) Form the pocket.

5. Make a ball out of half a sheet of newspaper. Lay it on the bottom half of the slab. This will support the pocket while it dries. Fold the bottom half over this ball (fig. 4).

6. Using a texture tool, stamp the edges on the bottom half of the pocket. This will seal the edges nicely (fig 5).

7. Make hanging holes at the top of the pocket about ½ inch (13 mm) down from the top. Wiggle the tool (hole maker, pencil, or pin tool) to make the hole a little bigger than you want it to be. Check the back side of the pocket to make sure the hole is a good size there too! Clay shrinks as it dries and gets fired (fig. 6).

(5) Seal the sides.

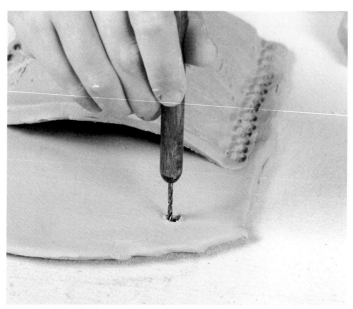

(6) Make holes for hanging the wall pocket.

8. Bisque fire the pocket when it is completely dry. Glaze with a low-fire glazes to bring out the design and texture you created. Fire again to finish (fig. 7).

(7) Glaze to bring out details.

KEEP GOING!

Wall pockets are wonderful for planting herbs outside. Attached to a porch or patio wall, they can be used to grow a whole garden of different herbs. But make sure to bring them inside when the temperature dips below freezing!

MEET THE ARTIST: STACEY ESSLINGER

Stacey Esslinger is an artist who works in porcelain. Her work is functional and incorporates textiles pressed into clay for texture. The textiles that Stacey uses for her pottery come from her family. Some are knitted sweaters, some are fancy embroidered linens, and others are from lace-patterned doilies her grandmother and other relatives made. She has a B.F.A. in ceramics from Alfred University and studied traditional ceramics in China. More about Stacey can be found at her website: www.staceyesslinger.com.

Vase by Stacey Esslinger

PINCH POT BIRDS

Before You Begin

Birds are animals that we often see right outside our window. They are fun to make out of clay in the pinch method as their bodies are naturally round. Check out a book on birds to get ideas for shape and color or use your imagination to sketch out a few ahead of time!

LET'S GO!

1. Begin with two balls of clay—one that fits easily in your hand and a second that is half the size or a little less than the first (fig. 1).

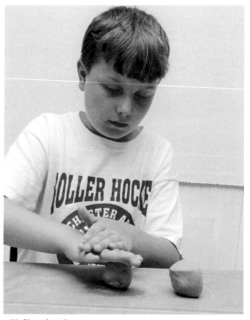

(1) Size the clay.

2. For the body, you will make a pinch pot with the larger ball of clay as you did in the earlier lesson in this chapter, but keep the opening as small as possible. When your pot is thin enough, make the opening smaller by pinching and folding it in (fig. 2).

(2) Almost close the hole.

3. Pinch the head into a smaller pot and form the opening in the same manner as the body of the bird. If the openings are similar in size, it is easier to put them together (fig. 3).

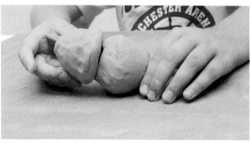

(3) Check the sizes.

4. Score both of the pots at the rims to join them together. Use your tool dipped in water to make a nice slurry of mud (fig. 4).

(4) Score the pots.

5. Work the two pieces together. Using your finger, gently (remember they are hollow!) smooth the joining line so the two separate pieces merge into one body (fig. 5).

(5) Smooth the body.

6. Roll out a third ball of clay (smaller than the head) for the wings. Use the slab method outlined in chapter 2 (fig. 6).

7. Using a pencil or rubber-tipped tool, draw a large oval on the slab. Cut the wingspan out with a knife (fig. 7).

8. With the scraps of clay left from the wings, make two eyes with two tiny balls of clay. Score and attach them to the head. Press them in with a pencil to make sure they are firmly attached (fig. 8).

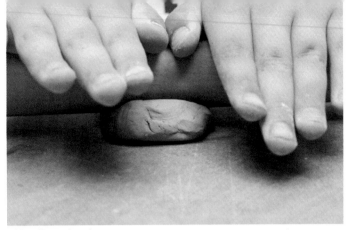

(6) Roll out the wings.

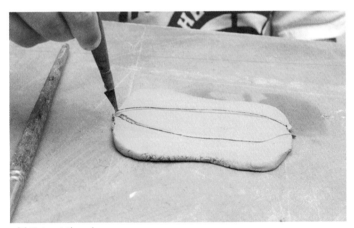

(7) Cut out the wings.

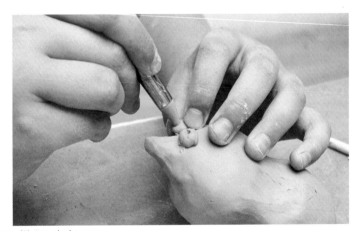

(8) Attach the eyes.

9. If desired add texture to the wings with a texture tool. Score the wings and the body adding water to the tool to make a firm connection (fig. 9).

(9) Add the wings.

10. Use a pin tool to poke a tiny hole in the underside of the bird to let the steam escape during the firing process (fig. 10).

11. Let the bird dry completely until it is no longer cool to the touch. Bisque fire the bird and then glaze. Fire again (fig. 11).

(10) Make a hole in the bottom of the bird.

KEEP GOING!

You can research birds in books published by the Audubon Society. Using the Audubon guides as references, try making the markings and colors of birds as realistic as possible.

(11) Glaze the bird.

BE INSPIRED

There were images and sculptures of birds in pre-Columbian times. These birds were made from similar clay to what you can use today. This bird is a sculpture, but also a whistle. Find out more about the Mayans and their culture at your local library.

SCULPTOR MEGAN BOGONOVICH

Ceramic sculptor Megan Bogonovich lives and works in Concord, New Hampshire. She is my friend and an amazing artist who inspires me and her students all the time. I asked Megan some questions and here's what she had to say.

What can you tell us about your beginnings as a maker?

I was a fort builder as a kid, a collector of outdoor stuff. Piles of acorns and crabapples, tree bark, goldenrod stems, petals, and vines. I have memories of cleaning up the pine needles to expose the earth floor. I was very interested in the feel of the moss and the dyeing possibilities of mashed-up berries. I know that I liked the arts and crafts projects of my childhood, but it was the tactile experimentation of being outdoors that I think most closely relates to my practice as an artist today.

How did you start making sculptures?

I knew I wanted to go to art school, but it took until my last year of college to know that I wanted to work with clay. My first ceramics class became an immediate obsession. It was all joy. It is nice to occupy three dimensions. Sculptures take up more space. You can look behind, under, through. Clay transforms. It starts out mushy and pliable and it become glassy and fragile. You make a precious thing … from mud. There are surprises in the kiln and such a variety of processes and techniques to play with.

What are your favorite materials to use?

Come on, clay!

Who are your favorite artists?

I love most artists. Museums make me happy and emotional. I am also inspired by commercial artists. I like the people who design costumes and sets, the people who make wallpaper and children's books. I also find actors, singers, and writers inspiring.

What was your proudest moment?

Tuesday, June 17, 1986, at 10:03.

As you can tell, Megan has a sense of humor. She teaches college students part time and works very hard most every day in her studio. She makes a lot of art, as you can see!

More information about Megan can be found at www.meganbogonovich.com

5 TEXTILES

Working with fabric, yarn, and other textile materials is very comforting and can feel quite grown-up for young artists.

It seems that fewer children today know how to handsew or knit than when I was young. It's exciting to watch a child thread a needle for the first time. It is empowering and a lifelong skill that can turn a simple piece of fabric into a work of art.

The most important thing to keep in mind when working with textiles is patience. Good lighting, comfortable chairs, and a relaxed atmosphere are all bonuses! Even if you are not skilled at sewing or weaving, the lessons presented here are accessible and fun. If you have no experience working with textiles, you might want to test out these lessons by yourself to gain insight and confidence. Keep in mind the joy of the process!

SOFT SCULPTURE

Before You Begin
Soft sculptures are fun ways to express yourself in animal, mineral, or vegetable form. We're taking our inspiration for this project from artist Claes Oldenburg, which means the sky is the limit! His famous Giant Hamburger sculpture is room-size and made from vinyl. What will you make?

MATERIALS

· sketch paper and pencil
· canvas or thick muslin
· cardboard or foam core
· masking tape
· permanent marker
· acrylic paint and paintbrushes
· straight pins
· scissors
· paint markers
· crewel embroidery needle
· embroidery floss
· fiberfill or kapok
· chopstick or dowel

LET'S GO!

1. Sketch out a few ideas on paper. It's good to have a few sketches to choose from (fig. 1).

2. Wrap your canvas or muslin over the cardboard or foam core and tape to the back (fig. 2).

3. Draw the front side of your idea on the fabric with pencil (fig. 3).

4. Go over your pencil lines with permanent marker (fig. 4).

(1) Sketch out ideas.

(2) Stretch the fabric.

(3) Draw idea on fabric.

(4) Use the marker.

83

(5) Paint the front of the sculpture.

(6) Cut out the sculpture.

(7) Add details.

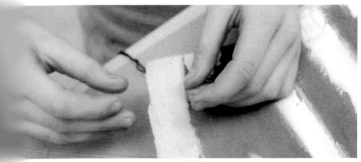

(8) Begin stitching.

5. Begin painting what will be the front of your sculpture with the acrylic paints (fig. 5). Let the paint dry.

6. When dry remove the front side from the cardboard and pin to another piece of fabric that is approximately the same size. Leave a 1-inch (2.5 cm) border around your outermost marker line and cut the two pieces out at the same time (fig. 6).

7. Remove the pins, tape the back side of your sculpture to the cardboard, and paint it. Let dry, and then remove from the cardboard.

8. Pin your front piece to your back piece with the painted sides out. Add details with the paint markers (fig. 7).

9. Thread the embroidery needle with about 12 inches (30 cm) of embroidery floss. Tie a knot on one end of the floss. Grasp the unknotted end of the floss in your dominant hand. Begin sewing from the back, bringing the needle up to the front at one side of the sculpture. Go slowly and make sure that you hang on to the unknotted end. Point your needle back down about ¼ inch (6 mm) from where you came up and push it through to the back. Down and up, down and up, almost all the way around (fig. 8).

10. Leave an open space for inserting the stuffing into your sculpture. Fill the farthest reaches of your sculpture first using a chopstick or dowel to reach small spaces. Continue to add stuffing until the sculpture has taken shape and seems full (fig. 9).

11. Sew the hole closed in the same manner as before (fig. 10).

(9) Stuff the sculpture

(10) Sew the sculpture closed.

KEEP GOING!

You can make an entire series of soft sculptures based on any subject! Think of storybook monsters, giants, trolls, gnomes, or perhaps a prince or princess. Fish make great sculptures too! One of my students even made a large hamburger as Claes Oldenburg did—the sky is the limit to what you can create!

MEET THE ARTIST: CLAES OLDENBURG

Claes Oldenburg is an American sculptor who is known for his large sculptures depicting common objects. Some of his pieces are soft sculptures made from vinyl. More about Claes Oldenburg can be found on the website for the Whitney Museum: www.whitney.org/ForKids/Collection/ClaesOldenburg.

NATURE WEAVING

Before You Begin

This weaving could easily live outdoors—whether in the garden or hanging from a tree or fence. It's also lovely to bring inside, but remember that the nature parts of this weaving will dry and be fragile. Indoors or out, it's a wonderful way to bring nature a little closer for observation and celebration! Go outside and gather your natural materials all at once or add to the weaving over a period of time.

LET'S GO!

1. Begin by measuring and cutting lengths of yarn or string a little longer than the length of your sticks for your warp (the vertical strings for your loom) (fig. 1).

(1) Cut the yarn.

2. Cut eight to ten 24-inch (61 cm)-long pieces of jute or strong string for the warp. Using a square knot (see chapter 1), tie the jute or string to one of the branches at intervals 1 to 2 inches (2.5 to 5 cm) apart (fig. 2).

3. Place the second branch about 20 inches (51 cm) from the first to make your loom. Tie the loose ends of the warps to the second branch (fig. 3). If it's easier, hang the loom on the wall to make adjustments. Branches are not overly straight, so a little "wonkiness" will occur!

MATERIALS

- two branches from a fallen tree each measuring 12 to 18 inches (30.5 to 46 cm)
- yarn
- scissors
- ruler
- jute or strong string
- assorted trims, ribbons, and yarns
- found nature items (bark, leaves, twigs, flowers, vines, moss, shells, plant stems, and any other interesting tidbits that you find)
- hot glue gun and glue sticks or tacky glue

(2) Tie the jute to one branch.

(3) Tie off the warp. *(4) Begin the weaving.*

(5) Weave around the end. *(6) Finish the weaving.*

4. Hang your loom from screws sticking out of a wall, or tie a string on either side of the top branch to hang it like a framed picture. Begin weaving at the bottom with a piece of ribbon or trim. Start by going over the first warp thread and then under the second, over the third, and so on. Leave a little overhang at the beginning to glue around the first thread to anchor it. If using yarn instead of ribbon or trim, you can simply tie it to the first warp thread (fig. 4).

5. Continue along your loom until your first piece of weft runs out. Tie on your next piece using a square knot. When you come to the end of the first row, wrap your yarn or trim around the end warp thread to secure it and continue back across the loom, weaving over and under (fig. 5).

6. Continue weaving up your loom until you are close to the top. We finished ours with a wide piece of seam binding. Glue the end or tie the end as you did at the beginning (fig. 6).

7. Take your collected nature items and weave over and under with them through the ribbon or yarn that you used earlier. For pinecones, acorns, and other rounded objects, you can tie or tuck them into place. Hot glue or tacky glue will keep them more secure.

8. Hang your nature weaving on an outdoor fence or garden wall! If you don't use glue to secure the found objects, you can swap them out or add to what's there anytime you'd like.

MEET THE ARTIST: PENELOPE DULLAGHAN

Penelope Dullaghan creates beautiful earth art pieces from nature. As an illustrator she uses 2-D materials to create her work. For her earth art, she focuses on out-of-doors, nature-based materials such as tree bark. Leaves, shells, stones, and moss all combine to create her composition. Photographing her earth art preserves it for others to see.

Earth art by Penelope Dullaghan

WOVEN WALL HANGING

Before You Begin

This lightweight, handmade weaving is both a loom and picture frame. The work you create will stay on the loom for display. You can use any combinations of fabric that you choose. If you have old T-shirts or other clothing, you can cut them into strips or use new fabric. Think about old sheets and linens too!

LET'S GO!

1. Begin by measuring off where the warp threads will go. Make a mark on the top and the bottom of your cardboard or foam core backing at every 1 inch (2.5 cm) starting 2 inches (5 cm) in from the side. End 2 inches (5 cm) in from the opposite side (fig. 1).

(1) Mark the warp threads with pencil lines.

2. Have an adult cut about a 1-inch (2.5 cm) slit on each of the lines on both ends of the cardboard or foam core. These slits will hold the warp thread.

3. Starting on the back, tape the end of the waxed linen right to the cardboard or foam core at the first slit. Wind the linen through the slit and over the front to the opposite end and through the slit. Keep wrapping the loom until you are at the end of the slits (fig. 2). Tape firmly to the back.

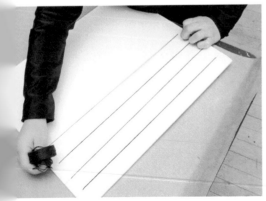

(2) Thread the loom.

(3) *Start to weave.*

(4) *Wrap the ends.*

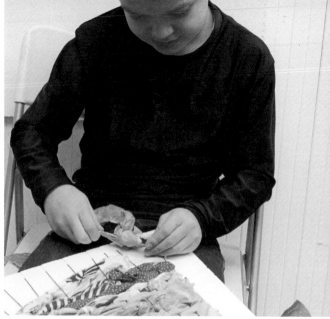

4. Begin to weave your first fabric strip by tying it onto the bottom left warp thread. Weave over and under the warp threads (fig. 3).

5. When you get to the last warp thread on your first row of weaving, wrap it around and start back across (fig. 4).

6. If you are at the end of your fabric strip, simply tie on your next fabric strip using the square knot method shown in chapter 1 (fig. 5).

(5) *Tie on a new strip.*

7. When you are finished with a few rows, "comb" down the fabric strips with your fingers to tighten the weaving.

8. When there is no more room to weave, simply tie off the last weft thread and hang your loom on the wall!

KEEP GOING!

You can make a very large loom and get all of your friends together to create a mural-size weaving. Just start with a giant box like one that a refrigerator comes in and make a really big pile of fabric strips!

MEET THE ARTIST: SUZANNE PRETTY

Suzanne Pretty is an artist from Maine who creates beautiful tapestries and other weavings. One of her earliest influences was her grandmother, who worked as a lady's tailor in London and was constantly knitting, crocheting, and sewing. "After graduating from Massachusetts College of Art with a B.A. in painting," Suzanne explains, "my work evolved from the texture of thick paint into quilted, stuffed, and painted pieces and then into tapestry. My interest in fiber reemerged." Learn more about Suzanne at www.suzannepretty.com.

Divided Landscape by Suzanne Pretty

STITCHED LANDSCAPE

Before You Begin
Embroidery can be a lot of fun. It makes your ideas and subjects rise up from the surface and glow with shiny floss. It takes some time to stitch even a small hoop's worth of landscape, so plan to work on this lesson over a few sittings. Be patient, and you will enjoy turning your threads into a landscape!

LET'S GO!

1. Place your hoop over your fabric and use the chalk to trace around the hoop (fig. 1).

2. Inside the circle draw a simple landscape with the chalk. Only make outlines. Your stitching will fill in the details (fig. 2).

3. Stretch the fabric with the hoop to prepare for stitching (fig. 3).

(1) Trace the hoop.

(2) Draw the landscape.

(3) Stretch the fabric.

MATERIALS

- 4- to 8-inch (10 to 20 cm) wooden embroidery hoop
- lightweight cotton or linen
- light-colored chalk
- assortment of embroidery floss
- embroidery needle
- scissors

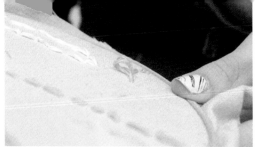

(4) Make your first stitch.

(5) Keep stitching.

(6) Take your time adding stitches.

4. Thread your needle with the embroidery floss and make a knot at the end. Have the "tail" of the unknotted end firmly grasped in your stitching or dominant hand.

5. Begin on the back side of the hoop and bring your needle up at the edge of a line in your drawing. Pull the floss all the way up to the knot. Now you will determine your stitch size. Keep your stitches approximately the same throughout; a good size to begin with is about ¼- or ⅛-inch (6 or 3 mm) long. Push your needle back through the top to the underside of your work. You have made your first stitch (fig. 4).

6. Continue following the line you made with the chalk with the stitch. When you get to the end of the line, fill in the rest of the area with stitches parallel with your first stitches. You can change colors of floss whenever you desire. Just leave a short tail on the back side so it doesn't pull through. Knot a new piece of floss and start where you left off (fig. 5).

7. Avoid stitches that are either too tight or so loose they get "loopy." Take your time and think about each stitch, and you will enjoy the process even more. Take a break when you need to (fig. 6).

8. When your landscape is as filled in as you like, cut the excess fabric close to the hoop for a tight finish. Or you can leave it as it is. You are the artist, so you decide.

KEEP GOING!

Why not try a landscape that includes a portrait of your home?

MEET THE ARTIST: LISA SOLOMON

Lisa Solomon is an artist from Oakland, California. Her book, *Knot Thread Stitch*, published by Quarry Books, is an inspiring collection of projects to stitch. Her fine artwork often contains thread and stitches and continues to amaze this author. You can see more of Lisa's work at: www.lisasolomon.com.

d.v. 7/28/70 embroidered fabric in hoop by Lisa Solomon

FROZEN JUTE SCULPTURE

Before You Begin

It's hard to imagine floppy string turning into a rigid sculpture, but with this project, you can make one or one hundred open-string spheres that hang from the ceiling. Think about where you would like to hang the finished sculpture because that will dictate how large it will be from the start. Decide too if you would like to sculpt a tiny bird to hang inside the sphere or prefer to leave it empty.

MATERIALS

- balloon
- jute
- scissors
- clear liquid glue
- stiff paintbrush
- waxed linen thread
- optional: glitter, acrylic paint, bake-at-home clay for bird

LET'S GO!

1. Blow up a balloon to the desired size of your sphere.

2. Cut lengths of jute long enough to wrap around your balloon. If they are too short, they won't stick well, and if they're too long, they will be hard to manage (fig. 1).

3. Drop the jute into the small container of clear glue. Use a stiff paintbrush to help adhere the glue to the jute (fig. 2).

(1) Cut the jute.

(2) Coat the jute with glue.

(3) Wrap the jute on the balloon.

(4) Finish the wrapping.

(5) Add glitter.

4. Wrap the jute around the balloon. Press the jute to itself wherever it overlaps on the surface (fig. 3).

5. Continue wrapping the jute, overlapping the string whenever possible (fig. 4).

6. When you have plenty of jute wrapped around the balloon, you can add glitter for some sparkle (fig. 5). You can also paint the jute with acrylic paint after it is dry.

7. While your sphere is drying, you can form a small bird if desired, out of the bake-at-home clay. It should be about the size to fit in your palm—just as shown in our student's hand at left.

8. Let the jute sphere dry for a day or two. Pop the balloon and carefully remove it. Hang the sculpture from the ceiling using the waxed linen thread.

KEEP GOING!

Try making a number of frozen string sculptures in different sizes and hang them together.

MEET THE ARTIST: ERIN SLINGSBY

As an emerging artist, Erin Slingsby enjoys mixing mediums, and she draws inspiration from various sources. With this set of work, which focuses on the shape of solar flares, she has appropriated imagery from studies in astronomy. These figures exhibit a sense of repetition in motion while maintaining an underlying structure. Erin re-creates these movements with natural materials such as wood and twine. Learn more about Erin at erinslingsby.wordpress.com.

Spheres by Erin Slingsby

MATERIALS

- dry forked branch
- assortment of trims, ribbons, threads, and thin fabric strips
- scissors
- optional: fishing line

BRANCH WRAPPING

Before You Begin

Nature comes indoors with this lesson and is dressed up with all the trimmings of a sewing room. What colors would you like your branch to be? Think rainbow or monochromatic or patterned. This sculpture can hang from the ceiling when you are done, so take a minute to think about where it will be displayed when choosing your colors.

LET'S GO!

1. Starting at the thick end of the branch (the part closest to the trunk), wrap and tie the first color of trim, ribbon, or other decorative strip with a square knot (fig. 1).

(1) Begin the wrapping.

(2) Add a new color.

2. Continue wrapping until you are ready to change colors. Tie on a new color using a square knot (fig. 2).

3. Don't worry about the knots because the ends can either be tucked in as you continue wrapping or left sticking out for a fun bowlike look. Keep wrapping (fig. 3).

4. When the branch is covered, select lengths of trim and tie them onto the branches so they hang down from the branch (fig. 4).

5. When you are finished with the hanging trims, attach three pieces of trim or fishing line evenly along to the branch so it can be suspended from the ceiling.

(3) Keep wrapping.

(4) Hang trims.

KEEP GOING!

Your wrapped branch could be the beginning of a branch mobile. Select smaller branches to hang off of your larger base branch. Wrap the small branches in the same manner as your base and see how far you can go with your hanging sculpture!

MEET THE ARTISTS: CHRISTO AND JEANNE-CLAUDE

Husband and wife Christo and Jeanne-Claude were a team of artists who wrapped thirty-two trees for their *Verhüllte Bäume* (Wrapped Trees) exhibit. Each tree was wrapped with shiny polyester fabric from patterns made for each size tree. The fabric made patterns in the sky. All the materials were recycled at the end of the exhibit.

6 SCULPTURE

Sculpture is one of the most exciting forms to create when you are a child. From an early age, many children take their paper drawings and cut them out and prop them up "to give them legs" in the space around them. Every child loves to construct and create in the round—even with simple materials.

This chapter will guide you through different types of sculpture with good "jumping-off" places to further your exploration. These lessons often include extra time for drying before going on to the next step. Be patient and plan ahead. There is a great feeling of accomplishment to make something that you can see in three dimensions taking up space. It often will be the first feeling of success for those who struggle with 2-D media. Enjoy the process and the unique qualities of each student's work—and try a project out for yourself!

JUMBO MASKS

Before You Begin

Making a large wall mask is extremely fun. It takes time, both to construct and to let dry. Plan on a few work sessions to complete this adventure. To start your ideas flowing, you can do some sketches on paper. Keep in mind what emotion you wish to portray and how to position the mouth and the eyebrows to express happiness, sadness, surprise, or anger. Animal faces make good masks too! Having a clear idea before you begin makes the construction go more smoothly.

MATERIALS

- large cardboard box
- scissors
- assorted recycled cardboard tubes, plastic containers, and scrap cardboard
- masking tape
- flour, water, and bowl for making papier-mâché goo
- stack of newspaper
- white gesso
- large foam brush
- pint of house paint and paintbrush
- acrylic paint and small paintbrushes for adding detail
- assorted embellishments (glitter, buttons, felt, trims, yarn, feathers, etc.)
- hot glue gun and glue sticks

LET'S GO!

1. Cut the large cardboard box in half, either straight or on the diagonal for a mask that sticks out along the ridge of the nose as shown. This gives shape to the face (fig. 1).

2. Use the recycled tubes and cardboard to build up the features of your mask on the box. Tape them securely with the masking tape (fig. 2). This is called making your armature. Armatures are the skeletons of a sculpture.

3. Using the flour and water, mix up the papier-mâché paste, or "goo," as described in chapter 1. Drop a half sheet of newspaper into the goo and allow it to get soaking wet (fig. 3).

4. Squeeze out the excess goo and spread the paper over the prepared armature. Smooth out the paper as much as you can. If your paper is very wrinkly, your mask will have wrinkles—which can be good for sculpting elephants and older people (fig. 4).

(1) Use the box on the diagonal.

(2) Tape features on securely.

(3) Wet the paper.

(4) Cover the armature.

(5) Cover the entire mask and let dry.

(6) Paint the base color.

(7) Add details with acrylic paint.

5. When the entire mask is covered with newspaper, let it dry and repeat. Three layers of papier-mâché make for a strong mask (fig. 5).

6. Coat the mask with a layer of white gesso. Use a foam brush for ease of spreading. This seals and primes the surface for painting.

7. Using the house paint, paint the base color of your mask (fig. 6).

8. Using the acrylic paints, add details (fig. 7). This step makes your mask come alive! The colors you select will determine the mood or feeling your mask expresses.

9. Use hot glue to add embellishments such as glitter, buttons, felt, trims, yarn hair, and feathers, which give dimension and personality to your mask. Choose carefully which embellishments will really add something special to the mask before gluing (fig. 8).

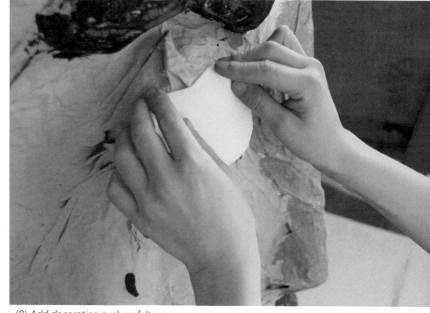

(8) Add decoration such as felt eyes.

KEEP GOING!

Making masks in a group can be a lot of fun. Plan a self-portrait mask-making session and hang them all up together! We did this at our local library and the masks greeted everyone who came in to the lobby.

BE INSPIRED

Carnival masks were the original inspiration for large-scale masks. Carnival is held before Lent in many areas around the world. The celebration can include parades and masks like those seen here.

2-D MEETS 3-D

Before You Begin

This lesson was brilliantly developed by my friend and fellow artist Amber Lavalley. Her idea was to take a masterwork still-life painting and make it 3-D. I think it is a wonderful way to introduce assemblage and art history to a student. For this example we chose Vincent van Gogh's *Sunflowers* painting. Having a reference for this lesson is most important. Choose a still-life painting with objects that you can re-create with simple materials, such as home-baked clay, recyclables, card stock, tissue paper, colored papers, tiny tin cans, and other accessible items.

MATERIALS

- cigar box or other small, shallow box
- clear liquid glue
- acrylic paint and paintbrushes
- tiny jar or tin can
- tissue paper (assorted colors)
- card stock
- pencil
- oil pastels
- scissors
- pin tool
- pipe cleaners
- bake-at-home clay
- optional: fabric scraps or felt

LET'S GO!

1. Begin by removing any loose paper from your box. Glue down any loose ends to make a smooth surface to paint. Choose a color for the outside of the box and paint it with a thick layer of acrylic paint (fig. 1).

2. After studying the masterwork, paint the inside with colors that will represent the still life's background and foreground (fig. 2).

3. For the van Gogh painting, we chose a tiny jar to cover in tissue to represent the ceramic vase in the painting. Glue the tissue on the jar using a brush and the clear glue (fig. 3).

(1) Paint the outside of the box.

(2) Paint the inside of the box.

(3) Glue the tissue to the jar.

103

(4) Detail the inside of the box.

(5) Draw the flowers.

4. Use a second color inside the box to represent the table. You could also use fabric or felt for this or for the background (fig. 4).

5. To create the sunflowers, draw on the card stock with pencil (fig. 5). Add vibrant color with oil pastels.

6. Cut out the flowers (fig. 6).

7. Poke two holes in the center of the flower with a pin tool or similar sharp tool (fig. 7). Add the pipe cleaner stem through the first hole and loop down the second to secure.

(6) Cut out the flowers.

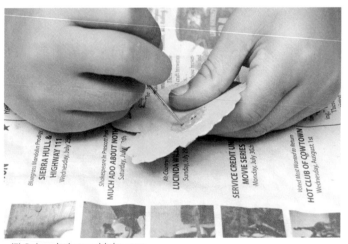

(7) Poke a hole to add the stem.

(8) Place the clay inside the jar.

(9) Arrange the flowers.

8. To secure the flowers in the vase, press a small ball of bake-at-home clay into the bottom of the jar (fig. 8).

9. Stick the flowers into the clay. You may have to trim some to make them fit as you would like. You can use your trimmings to make leaves (fig. 9).

MEET THE ARTIST: JOSEPH CORNELL

Joseph Cornell was considered the forerunner of Pop Art and assemblage. Prior to this, he had been embraced by the surrealist movement. He made films, assemblage, and installations. He was well known for his work in boxes entitled *Aviary*, which featured images of birds against a stark, white background. Find out more about Joseph Cornell online or at your local library.

Untitled (Dieppe) by Joseph Cornell, c. 1958

PLASTER RELIEF

Before You Begin

Set up a small still life with simple objects you have around your house. Make a drawing of your arrangement to acquaint yourself with the shapes and sizes of the objects. If you like, color it in with the watercolors for practice before starting the relief. If you're not happy with your first composition, try changing things around. Art is about practice, and the practice makes you feel better about your work.

LET'S GO!

1. Spread the joint compound over the wooden panel with the painting knife (fig. 1).

(1) Spread the joint compound.

MATERIALS

- joint compound (color-changing variety if possible)
- small wooden panel
- painting knife
- pencil
- watercolor paints
- water, jar, and paintbrush
- clear spray varnish (for use outside by an adult)

(2) Cover the panel.

(3) Draw in the compound.

2. Cover the panel thickly and completely. Work quickly as the compound dries fairly fast (fig. 2).

3. Draw into the compound with the knife or the eraser end of a pencil (fig. 3).

4. When you are finished, let the panel dry completely (fig. 4).

5. Using watercolors and a damp brush, paint your panel as you planned out first. Try not to use too much water as it can soften the compound (fig. 5).

6. Let the panel dry and spray finish it with a clear protective coating.

(4) Allow the panel to dry.

(5) Paint with watercolors.

MEET THE ARTIST: POLLY COOK

Polly Cook works in wall tile relief sculpture. Her work can range from small tiles as shown here to full wall-size murals many feet long. Her latest work is called *Love Stories*, and among other things she is inspired by poems of Byron, Shelley, and Keats. More of her work can be seen at: www.pollycook.com.

Man of Words *relief wall tile by Polly Cook*

PAPER MERPEOPLE

Before You Begin

Did you know that you can make newspaper, flour, and water into the tiniest or largest sculptures around? There is no limit to what you can make with these three ingredients. I am continually inspired by artist Carol Roll, who brings these three materials together in her sculptures. If you are not interested in merpeople, you can use this method to make other figures— just leave off the tail and make legs. Once you try this, you will find that you can make anything from papier-mâché!

LET'S GO!

1. Begin by opening a sheet of newspaper in front of you.

2. Roll the newspaper and twist it into a tube as shown. This step is the beginning of making an armature or skeleton for your sculpture (fig. 1).

3. Bend one of the ends over to form a head, and tape the neck in place tightly. Use as much tape as you need to make it secure (fig. 2).

(1) Twist newspaper into a tube.

(2) Tape the neck in place.

(3) Tape the body into shape.　　　(4) Tape the fins into shape.　　　(5) Roll a half sheet for each arm.

4. Now tape the body into shape. Give your merperson a waist with a band of tape (fig. 3).

5. When you get to the bottom of the tube, fan out both sides of the newspaper to create the fins. Tape them into place (fig. 4).

6. Roll up a half sheet of newspaper for the arms and tape each shut (fig. 5).

7. Tape the wrists to form hands. Add a band of tape in the middle to keep it all together (fig. 6).

8. Tape the arms to the body in the back and then crisscross the tape across the front (fig. 7).

(6) Tape off the hands.

(7) Tape the arms to the body.

109

9. Time for your papier-mâché strips. Use small strips with plenty of goo to begin. Keep the strips tight and smooth as you go (fig. 8).

10. It is important to keep the strips wet but not soaking wet. Scrape off the strips after dipping (fig. 9).

11. Use crisscross strips across the chest area and around the fins. Keep smoothing and keep adding strips to form the body and face (fig. 10).

12. Keep smoothing and wrapping the strips tightly. Mold the wet strips and form the hands and face a bit as you go. Let your figure dry after you have applied two layers of strips (fig. 11).

13. When your figure is completely dry, you can begin painting it with the acrylic paints (fig. 12).

(8) Begin wrapping the body.

(9) Scrape off the strips.

(10) Use crisscross strips.

(11) Wrap and smooth.

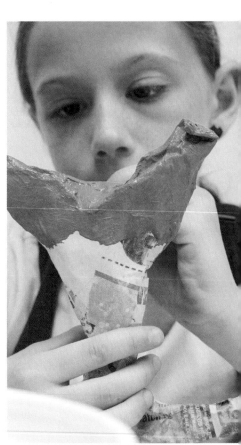

(12) Begin painting.

(13) Add details with the paint markers.

(14) Cut the yarn hair.

(15) Hot glue the hair bundles.

14. Use the paint markers for detailing the face, scales, and other features that you want to add (fig. 13).

15. Decide how long you want the hair to be and then cut the yarn into pieces that are just a little bit longer. Tie them into bundles (fig. 14).

16. Hot glue the bundles of yarn hair to the head. We used three bundles (fig. 15).

17. If you're making a mermaid, hot glue the shells on for her top. You can also add a paper or fancy ribbon crown to her head, and you can give her a tiny beaded necklace if you desire (fig. 16).

(16) Add a ribbon crown and necklace.

MEET THE ARTIST: CAROL ROLL

Carol Roll is an artist from Florida who creates impish, sweet, folk-art-type sculptures from papier-mâché. Her work is incredibly detailed, and the faces of her figures capture an incredible range of expressions from pouts to grins and more. For more information on Carol's work, visit www.nostalgicfolkart.com.

Queen of the Sea *by Carol Roll*

TINY PAPER ANIMALS

Before You Begin

Making a tiny animal sculpture can be both challenging and exciting! For these sculptures, it is best to have your animal in a resting position, either sitting or lying down on the base. Choose your animal to sculpt and an environment (base) for it to live on.

(1) Wet the towels.

MATERIALS

- paper towels
- flour, water, and bowl for making papier-mâché goo
- acrylic paint and assorted paintbrushes
- paint markers
- wood base
- tissue paper
- clear liquid glue
- optional: spray varnish

LET'S GO!

1. Begin with two squares of paper towels. Dip them into the papier-mâché goo and get them soaking wet (fig. 1).

2. Squeeze the excess goo out of the towels (fig. 2).

(2) Squeeze!

(3) Mold the paper towels.

(4) Add details.

(5) Paint your tiny animal.

3. Mold the wet compressed towels into the basic shape of your animal. Keep pressing the towels to shape them (fig. 3). Add more goo if needed.

4. Continue shaping wet paper towels into details such as eyes, beaks, fins, tails, and ears (fig. 4).

5. When your animal's body is complete, let the sculpture dry completely for a few days. Paint your animal with acrylic paint (fig. 5).

6. You can add details with small paintbrushes or paint markers (fig. 6).

7. Paint your wood base with acrylic paint. If you'd like, use the tissue paper to add details to the base for a textured ground covering or scrunched up in the shape of flowers or shrubs.

8. Glue your details and animal to the base (fig. 7). If you wish, use a spray varnish— but only outside and with an adult's help.

(6) Add details.

BE INSPIRED

A Japanese artist from the mid-nineteenth century created this netsuke sculpture of a tiger and two cubs. Often netsuke are tiny entwined animals with incredible detailing.

(7) Glue sculpture and details to the base.

PLASTER ASSEMBLAGE

Before You Begin

There are many artists who work in metal, plaster, and wood to create wall relief sculptures or assemblage. Louise Nevelson is one artist who created magnificent wall-size relief sculptures with wood pieces, found objects, and scraps. She often painted these works in a single color—often black or white or sometimes gold. Adam Pearson, the artist who inspired this lesson, creates wall relief sculptures with found metal objects and paint. Adam typically paints his entire work one color with a spot of bright color in a significant place. Find inspiration by arranging your found objects and think about the different ways you can put them together.

MATERIALS

- mat board
- assorted recycled materials (see materials list in chapter 2)
- scissors
- masking tape
- plaster cloth strips cut into 6-inch (15 cm) lengths
- bowl of water
- acrylic paint and paintbrushes

(1) Assemble materials on the mat board.

LET'S GO!

1. Arrange your materials on the mat board (fig. 1).

2. Cut any materials you need to make smaller with scissors (fig. 2).

3. After arranging the pieces, tape everything firmly to the board (fig. 3).

(2) Cut the pieces to size.

(3) Tape the pieces to the mat board.

4. Dip a strip of plaster cloth into the water. Get it completely wet and keep it flat (fig. 4).

5. Lay the strip over the objects and rub it smooth. Rub the strip until you no longer see any holes in the cloth and the object looks white (fig. 5).

6. Cover all the elements in your relief sculpture. Make sure to rub the strips to activate the plaster and to smooth the surface (fig. 6).

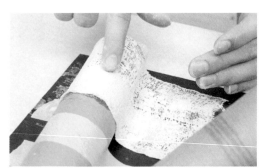

(5) Rub the plaster strips.

(4) Dip the plaster strips in water.

(6) Cover all the elements.

7. Paint your relief sculpture one color if desired (fig. 7).

8. Or paint it many colors (fig. 8).

(7) Paint the sculpture all one color.

(8) Paint the sculpture many colors.

MEET THE ARTIST: ADAM PEARSON

Adam is a Barrington, New Hampshire, sculptor and craftsman who received his bachelor of fine arts degree from the University of New Hampshire. He uses found metals for his sculptures and a variety of materials for his functional work. Find out more about Adam at www.pearsonsculpture.com.

Relief panel by Adam Pearson

LITTLE WORLDS

Before You Begin

These little worlds are one part snow globe, one part tiny art installation. You can decide first what your scene is going to be. Imagine yourself standing inside this tiny world: What would you see? Collect the things you would see or would like to see inside your tiny world. Gather some fallen branches and ask an adult to cut them into chunky 1- to 3-inch (2.5 to 8 cm)–high pedestals. Raid the toy box for tiny figurines, both human and animal, or look for them in hobby shops. If you desire, you can use polymer clay to make your own creatures that will live in your little world!

MATERIALS

- branch stump cut from tree limb
- tiny plastic or glass animals or polymer clay to make your own
- artificial plants for trees or shrubs for woodland worlds
- acorns, pinecones, and other found objects from nature
- tiny pebbles and sea glass
- shells, sand, and glitter for seaside worlds
- cotton balls and glitter for snowy worlds
- assortment of dried mosses
- floral putty
- hot glue gun and glue sticks
- optional: stemless wine glass for a vitrine

BE INSPIRED

This lesson was inspired by the art of Joseph Cornell. I thought it would be fun to mix Cornell's found-object work with the tiny enclosure of the branch stump.

(1) Arrange the scene.

(2) Add the animal.

LET'S GO!

1. Begin by assembling your little world's components. Put floral putty under each component that you add to your stump. Move them around until you are pleased with the scene (fig. 1).

2. Make sure that you don't add too many objects! Place your animal or creature inside too (fig. 2).

3. If you're using a stemless wine glass to cover your scene (like a hood over your world), check that it will fit over what you have added to the stump. The components should easily fit inside the glass and not stick out the sides (fig. 3).

4. If you need more "sticking power" for your items, use a small amount of hot glue in addition to the putty.

5. Put on the glass cover and set on a shelf to enjoy (fig. 4).

(3) Fit the glass over the scene.

(4) Display your finished little world.

KEEP GOING!

Pick one setting—the mountains? your backyard?—and try making a different world for each of the four seasons.

The fog comes
on little cat feet.

It sits looking
over harbor and city
on silent haunches
and then moves on.

Carl Sanburg

POETRY BOX

Before You Begin

When you make a piece of art inspired by someone else's art, it's called *ekphrasis* (it's a Greek word). In our gallery we have had three exhibits of visual art that was inspired directly from poetry. For this lesson, you will begin with a poem and create a sculptural work from that poem.

LET'S GO!

1. Either handwrite or print a poem you like on white card stock that is sized to fit inside the lid of the cigar box. Then sketch out some ideas for illustrating the poem.

2. Cover your cigar box with the decorative papers. We used pages from a discarded dictionary. Use the glue stick and plenty of pressure to adhere the pages to the box (fig. 1).

(1) Cut the paper covering to fit.

MATERIALS

- selected poem
- card stock, white and colored
- cigar box
- assorted decorative papers
- glue stick
- scissors
- pencil
- colored pencils
- oil pastels
- polymer clay
- hot glue gun and glue sticks
- large beads made of wood, plastic, or glass
- optional: watercolor set and paintbrushes

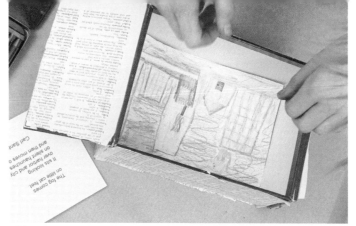

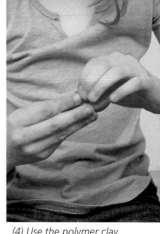

(2) Illustrate the poem.

(3) Glue down the illustration.

(4) Use the polymer clay.

3. Cut a piece of card stock to fit inside the bottom of the box. Trace around the box with a pencil to get the right size.

4. Illustrate your poem using colored pencils and oil pastels on the paper you just cut out. It will serve as a background in your box (fig. 2).

5. Glue the illustration inside the bottom of the box (fig. 3).

6. If desired, use watercolor paints to add more color to the papers covering the box or to the illustration. Glue your poem to the inside of the lid.

7. Create additional elements for your poetry box with the polymer clay. Bake the clay as directed on the package. For our poem, we created a tugboat (fig. 4).

8. Finish by hot gluing large beads for a handle to open your box lid

KEEP GOING!

Ask a friend to write a poem and you can surprise him or her by making a poetry box from that poem. Or make up a poem yourself!

BE INSPIRED

Much art has inspired other art through the ages. The poetry of Carl Sandburg is a good place to start for poems that will inspire your sculptures. Find poetry books by Carl Sandburg and other poets at your local library.

METAL SCULPTOR ADAM PEARSON

Adam Pearson is a New Hampshire–based sculptor who has a keen eye for finding beauty in the decayed and discarded. His sculptures have graced our galleries and have been placed in public venues as well as many personal gardens. I have followed Adam's career since his BFA work at the University of New Hampshire. His ability to create something from seemingly nothing is amazing. I am proud to own one of his earlier works, which lives in our garden and delights us year-round with its fluid lines and rusty color.

What can you tell us about your beginnings as a maker?
I remember, as a kid, having fun building things, using tools, scrounging for materials, and just making stuff. When I was old enough, I went to work for my father doing construction. I have always enjoyed landscaping and moving rocks and dirt around. For me, sculpture gives the opportunity to explore the best parts about these different experiences I had growing up and lets me use any of the possible mediums I am drawn to.

How did you start making sculptures?

My early inspiration for making sculpture came primarily from trying to emulate the work of Andy Goldsworthy. Balancing rocks and working with found materials was a way for me to combine aspects of landscape design and construction and to present the end product through photography and sculpture.

What are your favorite materials to use?

Steel, but really just about any metal, both found and/or fabricated. I also enjoy using clay, wood, and stone when I get the chance.

Who are your favorite artists?

Historically, David Smith and Julio Gonzalez. Also Andy Goldsworthy, as noted above, and many others, including artists, crafters, furniture makers, and architects.

What was your proudest moment?

To date, the birth of my daughter. But any time I sell a sculpture, I am proud to know that it is appreciated by someone else.

More Information about Adam can be found at www.pearsonsculpture.com

7 JEWELRY

Making jewelry is part craft, part art, and a big part fun. These lessons use inexpensive materials and simple techniques to blend fine art inspiration with something you can make to give as a special gift or to wear yourself. It takes a little practice to get used to handling some of the tools and the tiny beads, but it's exciting to have a unique bracelet or new pair of earrings at the end of the session!

When working with groups of children, I would suggest starting with paper beads, which use their hands as the main tool, and moving on to the wire bending after they have built up their confidence. Clay beads are terrific for large groups to design and string colorful necklaces. Most of these lessons can be adapted to other kinds of jewelry—for instance, the paper beads can be made into bracelets by using elastic string or combined with the clay beads for a different kind of necklace. I encourage my students to experiment, and I hope that you bring your own ideas to these lessons!

PAPER BEAD NECKLACE

Before You Begin

Choose a color scheme from the pages of a magazine. Any color or set of colors works, so maybe you can pick a rainbow or settle on one or two main colors. You are the artist, so you get to decide. The plastic or wood beads that you choose to go in between your paper beads can coordinate with the color scheme as well.

LET'S GO!

1. Begin by cutting out long triangles of colored magazine pages as shown (fig. 1).

2. When you have a good stack of triangles, you can begin rolling them. Start at the wide end of the triangle and roll the paper over a toothpick (fig. 2).

(1) Cut out triangles.   *(2) Begin rolling.*

MATERIALS

- colorful magazine pages
- scissors
- toothpicks
- clear liquid glue
- Styrofoam tray
- assortment of small and medium-size beads
- waxed linen cord

3. When you come to the end of the paper, put a dot of clear glue over the end of the paper and spread over the paper bead to seal. Try to avoid sealing the toothpick to the bead (fig. 3).

4. Stick the toothpick with the bead into a Styrofoam tray to allow it to dry (fig. 4).

5. When the beads are dry, you are ready to string them on the cord. Measure the cord around your neck and cut to the length you prefer. Tie a knot at one end (fig. 5).

6. Begin stringing your beads in whatever pattern you've chosen. Alternate between the paper beads and the purchased beads. When your linen cord is full, tie the ends together and try on your necklace (fig. 6).

(3) Glue the bead.

(4) Dry the beads.

(5) Measure the cord.

(6) Try on the necklace.

KEEP GOING!

Try making several necklaces and tie them together to make a necklace with multiple strands. Make a large focal bead to keep the strands together.

BE INSPIRED

During Victorian times in England, women often gathered to make paper beads. Much like the ones that are made today, they made beads from newsprint or discarded book pages. These women, however, did not use the beads to make necklaces; instead, they strung the beads for curtains or room dividers. Today people all over the world make paper beads for jewelry.

MODERN CAMEO PIN

Before You Begin

Cameos are images of pretty women cut into stones. For our cameo pin, we will use a simple drawing and a selection of tiny beads. It's a cameo with a twist! Use a photograph or magazine image if you would like a reference or inspiration for your drawing.

LET'S GO!

1. Start by making an oval or circle on the card stock the size that you want your pin to be. Use a pencil to draw a simple face on the card stock. Do not add details to your face as they will be lost in the beading process. It is enough to have one line for the eyes, one for the nose, and one or two for the lips (fig. 1).

2. Begin adding the beads. Drop small amounts of clear glue on the drawing. Drop a bead into the glue where the mouth, nose, and eyes are. Next add beads to the face for the skin and hair. The colors can be anything you desire—they don't even have to be realistic! Continue to fill in the background with beads (fig. 2).

MATERIALS

- card stock
- pencil
- seed beads and bugle beads
- clear liquid glue
- scissors
- Styrofoam tray
- dimensional glue
- felt
- tacky glue
- hot glue gun and glue sticks
- pin back

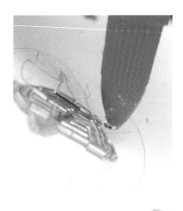

(1) Draw the face.

(2) Glue the beads.

(3) Cut out the cameo.

(4) Add the coating.

(5) Add felt.

(6) Add a pin back.

3. Let the glue dry completely (overnight is best) and then cut around the edge of the cameo (fig. 3).

4. Place the cameo on the Styrofoam tray. Squeeze the dimensional glue one drop at a time over the entire face of the cameo. Do not squeeze too hard or rush the process! When the cameo is covered with glue, let it dry overnight (fig. 4).

5. When the cameo is dry, cut out a felt backing the same size as the cameo. This will give structure to the pin and cover the paper. Glue on the felt with tacky glue (fig. 5).

6. When the tacky glue is dry, hot glue a pin back to the back of the cameo (fig. 6). Wear your cameo with pride!

KEEP GOING!

Try making a cameo in the likeness of your best friend or a relative. This might be more challenging but also more fun!

BE INSPIRED

Cameos have been made for centuries to capture a wide range of images from pretty maidens to powerful rulers. This exquisite cameo depicts a king.

POP ART EARRINGS

Before You Begin

These earrings are a throwback to the Pop Art movement. If you look at a book on Pop Art, you'll see that bold graphics and everyday items were big parts of what the movement was all about. So choose your favorite object to reproduce in a tiny drawing for your earrings.

MATERIALS

- 1-inch (2.5 cm) hole punch
- white and colored card stock
- pencil
- colored pencils
- scissors
- self-sealing laminate pockets
- hammer and small nail
- piece of wood to nail on
- jump rings
- ear wires
- needle-nose pliers

LET'S GO!

1. Punch out a circle to make a pattern using the 1-inch (2.5 cm) hole punch (fig. 1). Trace the circle onto the card stock (fig. 2).

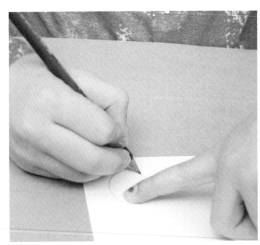

(1) Punch out a circle.

(2) Trace the circle.

2. Using the circle's outline as your guide, create your design inside the circle with the colored pencils. You can reference Andy Warhol, Roy Lichtenstein, or other Pop artists if you need some inspiration (fig. 3).

(3) Draw the design.

3. Cut down the size of the card stock to about 2 x 3 inches (5 x 7.5 cm) (fig. 4).

4. Using the 1-inch (2.5 cm) hole punch, cut out the circles you designed.

5. Using the 1-inch (2.5 cm) hole punch, cut out colored card stock for the back side of your earrings if desired.

6. Open the laminate pockets and place the colored paper circles on the sticky laminating paper. Put the drawings faceup on top of the colored circles, which will act as a colorful back side to the drawings you created. Close the pouch to seal (fig. 5).

(4) Cut down the card stock.

(5) Laminate the circles.

(6) Press firmly.

7. Press firmly to set (fig. 6).

8. Cut the circles out around the outside of the air pocket that surrounds the paper inside the laminate. If you cut into the little gap, you can glue it shut with clear liquid glue (fig. 7).

9. Using a hammer and small nail, pound a hole through the top of the circle, close to but not touching the edge (fig. 8).

(7) Cut out the circles.

(8) Make a hole.

10. Open a jump ring by twisting it side to side—do not stretch it open. Slip it through the hole you made in the laminated paper. Make sure it faces the front. Slip on the ear wire and close the jump ring (fig. 9).

11. Put on your earrings and smile (fig. 10).

(9) Add the ear wires.

(10) Wear your finished earrings!

BE INSPIRED

Pop Art is one of the most colorful and dynamic art movements, and the work it produced baffled people, outraged people, and made others laugh. Visit your local library to see books on Pop Art and get inspired by Andy Warhol, Roy Lichtenstein, Jasper Johns, and Jim Dine.

KEEP GOING!

You can make artsy earrings from any period of history in this fashion. You could even turn your favorite doodle of the day into jewelry! Campbell's Soup cans like Andy Warhol painted could be fun too.

CLAY BEAD NECKLACE

Before You Begin

Making beads for a necklace is a fun way to create something beautiful for yourself—or a gift for someone special. When you select your colored clays, think about the colors of glass beads as they will be strung next to the ones you make yourself. Choose a variety of colored clay so you can change your mind as you go. We are going to make round clay beads, but there is no limit to the shapes you can create.

MATERIALS

- nonstick surface to work on (we used a cutting board)
- bake-at-home clay
- wooden skewer
- pipe cleaner
- small glass beads
- waxed linen

LET'S GO!

1. Bake-at-home clay is usually stiff when you first open the package. Break it into small pieces and warm it up in your hand (fig. 1).

(1) Break the bake-at-home clay into pieces.

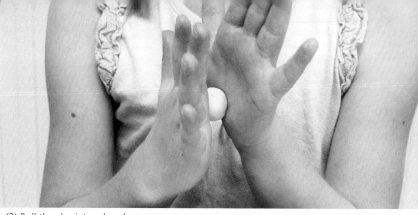

2. Once the clay is warm, begin rolling it into a bead shape (fig. 2).

3. You can add little pieces of another color of clay to decorate the beads (fig. 3).

4. Make small and large beads for variety in your necklace (fig. 4).

(2) Roll the clay into a bead.

(3) Add other colors.

(4) Create different sizes and shapes.

(5) Make holes with the skewer.

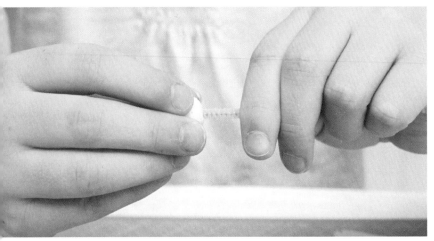

(6) Use a pipe cleaner for small beads.

(7) Arrange the beads.

5. When you are done making the beads, begin making holes in them so you can string them later. Use the skewer for the larger beads (fig. 5).

6. Use the pipe cleaner if the bead is small (fig. 6). Bake as instructed.

7. Arrange the beads for your necklace, with a glass bead or two if desired, on either side of your handmade beads (fig. 7).

8. Cut the waxed linen to a length that fits easily over your head plus half as much again. Tie a knot at one end (fig. 8) and string a glass bead on, adding a little bead first.

(8) Tie the knot.

9. String your beads in the order that you have laid out (fig. 9). Tie the ends together with a square knot and wear it proudly!

(9) Wear your beads.

MEET THE ARTIST: MEGAN BOGONOVICH

Megan Bogonovich makes everything out of clay. Even these giant beads. They are decorative and huge! More information about Megan can be found at www.meganbogonovich.com.

Giant beads by Megan Bogonovich

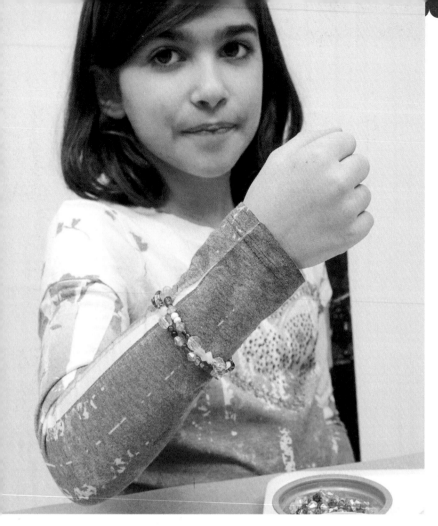

MEMORY WIRE BRACELET

Before You Begin
Think about what sort of pattern you might like to make with the beads that you have. Old necklaces and bracelets are wonderful for recycling into new jewelry. You can buy new beads too.

MATERIALS

- memory wire cut to wrap around your wrist two or three times
- assortment of beads
- round-nose pliers

LET'S GO!

1. Make a small twist at one end of the memory wire. It is a hard wire, so an adult can be helpful with this step (fig. 1).

(1) Bend the end of the wire.

2. Start to thread your beads onto the wire in the pattern of your choice (fig. 2).

3. When the wire is almost full, take the round-nose pliers and bend the end of the wire into a small circle that will hold the beads onto the wire. Twist or bend the end of the wire halfway around to form a circle and then bend it the rest of the way around to complete the circle (fig. 3).

(2) Thread the beads.

(3) Bend the end.

KEEP GOING!

You can make memory wire bracelets with the clay beads you made earlier in this chapter. Each bead should be small enough to fit on the wire easily. You can make sure that the holes in your beads are the right size by slipping them on the wire before baking them.

BE INSPIRED

This rainbow wrap bracelet was made by Chumisa Manyamalala, an artist in South Africa who makes beautiful jewelry with tiny beads. She belongs to a collective of talented beading artists who live in the country's Kljoe region. I found their beautiful work through an organization called Art Aids Art. You can see and learn more about their work at www.lovingafrica.com and www.artaidsart.org.

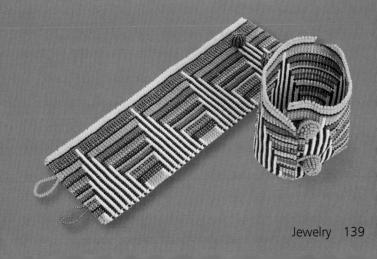

JEWELER
JANE ESLINGER

Jane Eslinger is an artist who makes jewelry and small metal sculptures. She is also a wonderful seamstress and makes lovely origami animals. She made fifty beautiful paper birds for my wedding—and most of the guests still have them! I stopped by her studio and asked her some questions about her life as an artist.

What can you tell us about your beginnings as a maker?
As long as I can remember, I have been making things. When I was a kid, I made clothes for my troll collection, but I also was always taking the wheels off my doll carriages and building go-carts. The first one was called Thunderbird after a TV show at the time. It was red and white and went like a rocket—no brakes, though, which was the first design problem I ever faced. Thunderbird 2 was a big improvement in the control department!

How did you start making jewelry?
I had been making books and working with paper in sculpture and origami when I started to wonder: Since metal is flat like paper, is it possible to do metal origami? So I enrolled in a basic jewelry-making class to learn some techniques and how to work with metals. I did make some origami flowers in metal, but I ended up really enjoying the

tools and the process of metalworking, so I just kept going and learning more. Now it's a few years on and I still love it. The techniques are simple and easy to learn, but what you do with them is all about your aesthetic, and the sky's the limit as far as that goes!

What are your favorite materials to use?
I like to use recycled and repurposed copper that I cut, file, hammer, and raise into various shapes, but I also love color and wanted to find a way to incorporate it into my work without using gems and beads. I was so excited when I discovered enamels! There are so many beautiful colors out there, and I can sift the powders or paint them right onto the copper and then fire using either a kiln or my acetylene torch. There's such a rich history of enamel work to explore too.

Who are your favorite artists?
Gustav Klimt, Alexander Calder, and Wolf Kahn.

What is your proudest moment?
Whenever I see someone on the street wearing one of my pieces of jewelry, I am tickled pink!

More information about Jane can be found at www.janeeslinger.com.

RESOURCES FOR MATERIALS

Australia
Eckersley's Arts, Crafts,
and Imagination
(store locations in New
South Wales, Queensland,
South Australia, and Victoria)
www.eckersleys.com.au

Canada
Curry's Art Store
Ontario, Canada
www.currys.com

DeSerres
www.deserres.ca

Michaels
www.michaels.com

Opus Framing & Art Supplies
(Stores in Vancouver,
Langley, Kelowna, and
Victoria, B.C.)
www.opusframing.com

France
Graphigro
Paris, France
www.graphigro-paris11.fr

Italy
Vertecchi
Rome, Italy
www.vertecchi.com

New Zealand
Littlejohns Art & Graphic
Supplies Ltd.
Wellington, New Zealand

United Kingdom
T N Lawrence & Son Ltd.
www.lawrence.co.uk

Creative Crafts
www.creativecrafts.co.uk

United States
A. C. Moore
www.acmoore.com

Ampersand Art Supply
www.ampersandart.com

Baily Pottery Supply
www.bailypottery.com

Big Ceramic Store
www.bigceramicstore.com

Daniel Smith
www.danielsmith.com

Dick Blick
www.dickblick.com

Jo-Ann Fabric and
Craft Stores
www.joann.com

Michaels
www.michaels.com

Sheffield Pottery Supply
www.sheffield-pottery.com

Utrecht
www.utrechtart.com

CONTRIBUTING ARTISTS

Megan Bogonovich
www.meganbogonovich.com
Polly Cook
www.pollycook.com
Cada Driscoll
cadacreates.blogspot.com
Penelope Dullaghan
www.penelopedullaghan.com
Jane Eslinger
www.janeeslinger.com
Stacey Esslinger
www.staceyesslinger.com
Jane Kaufmann
www.janekaufmann.com
Jeanne McCartin
Portsmouth, New Hampshire
Adam Pearson
www.pearsonsculpture.com
Suzanne Pretty
www.suzannepretty.com
Carol Roll
www.nostalgicfolkart.com
Erin Slingsby
erinslingsby.wordpress.com
Gail Smuda
www.gailsmuda.com
Lisa Solomon
www.lisasolomon.com

Thank you!

The 3-D Art Lab Kids: Liam, Robbie, Grace, Isaac, Caanan, Nora
Charlotte, Owen, Natalie, Ethan, Lara, Gabbe, Miles, Sadie

ABOUT THE AUTHOR

Susan Schwake is an artist, art educator, and curator. She actively exhibits her work in galleries around the United States and Europe and sells her work online and in her own gallery, artstream. Susan has been part of juried public art exhibitions, creating large-scale, site-specific works. Her passion for teaching and making art with others grew from a tiny seed of an idea in the fourth grade. Working in such diverse settings as schools, community centers, special needs nonprofits, summer camps, intergenerational facilities, libraries, and her own little art school, Susan has taught art to hundreds of people over the past twenty years.

She created a permanent exhibition of children's art, involving more than one hundred local children, that graces the walls of a new children's room in her local library in 1997 and refreshed it in 2007 to celebrate its tenth anniversary. In 2000, she directed a similar project with four hundred people in an intergenerational setting for a new multi-agency facility, bringing the staff, families, and clients more closely together through the process of making art. She has enjoyed many residencies in public and private schools, with whole school projects, and in special needs groups and single classrooms. Since the release of her first book, *Art Lab for Kids*, Susan has offered workshops to parents and teachers and student teachers at universities, art studios, and schools. She enjoys sharing her methods and learning from others.

In 2005, Susan began a blog called artesprit. Through the blog, she embraced writing and photographing her world, meeting many new artists and friends around the globe. She co-owns and is the curator for artstream studios in New Hampshire. She enjoys bringing compelling group shows of contemporary art to her corner of New England. She is happy to be working alongside her husband every day doing what she loves most. Follow her adventures:

Blog: www.artesprit.blogspot.com
Website: www.susanschwake.com
Gallery: www.artstreamstudios.com

ACKNOWLEDGMENTS

Thanks to everyone who touched this book—from my incredible students to everyone at Quarry!

To my beautiful family, who gives me so much love, joy, patience, support, and creative inspiration every day. I love you!